# OVERCOMING ADVERSITY

# *Retreat/Companion* WORKBOOK

### RICHARD T. CASE

# Acknowledgments

We wish to thank all of the leaders of our **Ministry: Living Waters—ABIDE Ministries!** These leaders have also learned what it means to live in this world of adversity (we all the time get to have them bear witness to God's faithfulness in overcoming their adversity)—and as they have learned the depth of this critical part of the Christian life, they now are all giving this away to others—who then are learning to have adversity overcome, and thus, it is exponentially multiplying. Thank you all:

**These leaders are:**

Jake & Mary Beckel
Joe & Leigh Bogar
Rich & Janet Cocchiaro
Larry & Sherry Collet
Scott & Kristen Cornell
David & Melissa Dunkel
Tom & Susanne Ewing
Rick & Kelly Ferris
Joel & Christina Gunn
Scott & Terry Hitchcock
Chris & Jaclyn Hoover
Rick & Nancy Hoover
Tad & Monica Jones
Ed & Becky Kobel
Don & Rachelle Light
Chris & Heidi May
Terry & Josephine Noetzel
Steve & Carolyn Van Ooteghem
Preston & Lynda Pitts
Dan & Kathy Rocconi
Bob & Keri Rockwell
John & Michelle Santaferraro
Allyson & Denny Weinberg
Neal & Kathy Weisenburger

*OVERCOMING ADVERSITY RETREAT/COMPANION WORKBOOK*
PUBLISHED BY LIVING WATERS—ABIDE MINISTRIES
7615 Lemon Gulch Way
Castle Rock, CO 80108



ISBN: 978-1-7360588-7-9


Publisher's Cataloging-in-Publication data

Names:
Title:
Description: .
Identifiers: ISBN | LCCN
Subjects:


Printed in the United States of America 2024 — 2nd ed

# TABLE OF CONTENTS

# INTRODUCTION

# INTRODUCTION

Almost all Christians have much confusion about God's goodness and how that goodness relates to their  personal experience of adversity (things not going well in their life). They view life through their difficult experiences, and thus, their real (true in their soul) perspective is that God is really not that good. This is based on faulty understanding of God and our life here in this world. They have been taught:

1. God is in control of everything.

2. Thus, God is in control of my life.

3. Which means, everything that happens to me is God's will. Since He is in control, whatever happens to me must be His will.

4. Lots of very difficult things have happened to me, are happening to me, and it looks like it's not getting better; or when things do get better, another difficult thing happens right behind it. This is certainly not the wonderful life that I had planned out or thought was going to happen, especially being a believer and a child of God.

5. Thus, it appears that others have God's favor and blessing that is spoken of in Scripture, but not me.

6. The only conclusion that can be drawn (not said in the intellect or to others, since that is not what Christians are supposed to say) is that God just is not that good, or at least not to me. Why does all this bad stuff happen in the world, and especially to me, if He is in control? No matter how much I try to say, "This must be God's will for my own good, and I am supposed to live with it." We call this Christian fatalism; it is something my heart just cannot accept (and rightly so).

7. So, underneath it all, there is a deep disappointment with God, a degree of anger and resignation. This, then, results in me not having an intimate relationship with God through abiding in the Word, through prayer, and in the Spirit. Why bother? It does not seem to matter. Further, the best thing I can do is work really hard with my best thinking to try to overcome my adversities

and hope that God does some things to help me. Though, if things do seem to get better, I do not expect this to last. I will pray, put on the smiling Christian face and say things are fine, but I do not really expect answers to prayers and will likely continue to have difficulty.

This has been a strategic trick of the enemy. The very conclusions we reach and the acceptance of the adversity as normal actually serves to perpetuate our adversity. We do know there is an enemy, but since God is in control and has gained victory over principalities and powers at the cross, does He not have the ability to keep the enemy away from my life? Is there any hope at all, or are we just to accept this very difficult life as normal? Should we accept that we are sinners and are going to fail, that bad things happen, and that God uses it all to teach us things? Or, do we see God as not very good, someone who seems cruel and unwilling to take better care of His children? Are we just supposed to put up with adversity as a way of life and as Christians are relegated to this life, and this is all part of God's will? Are adversity and suffering just a way that God is teaching us things, particularly to be sanctified, meaning the harder the lesson the more sanctified I will become? This, to us, seems long and hard, especially if we aren't sure we are learning a lesson (especially since we tend to repeat it).

This course will take us through the Word to help us see the truth that God is absolutely good! He has wonderful plans for us. We will experience adversity. Some is normal, as the Bible tells us that in this world, we will have trouble. Some is from God, but much is not. The good news is that there are remedies for all of them; and we need to learn exactly what it is, what are the sources and causes, and how we are to overcome adversity in our lives.

Adversity did not just come upon mankind as part of God's original plan. Rather, it came upon us as a result of the *Fall of Adam and Eve*, who exercised their self-will, disobeyed God's instruction to not eat of the tree of the Knowledge of Good and Evil, and died as God had warned (meaning the Holy Spirit departed from their nature). As a result, Satan gained authority and power over this Earth; and this power is pure destruction, designed to steal, kill, and destroy. Adversity came about because of man's selfishness and the opposing power of Satan that is now operating where things are difficult, painful, frustrating, hard, annoying, oppressive, confusing, etc. Adversity now is normal and ever present.

## REVIEW: GOD'S ORIGINAL PLAN FOR MANKIND

God's original plan for mankind is recorded in Genesis 1 and 2, which were written before the Fall. He set forth the exceptional life that Adam and Eve enjoyed before the Fall, which was His original plan. In chapters 2 and 3, it is revealed what life with Him looks like after the Fall. This exceptional life included these seven exceptional gifts:

1. Exceptional Authority: Victory and Power to Loose and Bind

Authority is defined in the Scriptures as dominion and power manifested in many different ways:

- Splendor, majesty, beauty, vigor, glory
- In-charge, control, have jurisdiction, power to influence, cause to become
- Great, much; many; enlarged, exceedingly abundant
- Power (physical and spiritual) of doing the supernatural
- Right to govern, rule, command (possessing authority)
- Mighty work, strength, miracle
- Performing miracles
- Excellence

> "All authority emanates from Him, as He is and has the ultimate authority, which is the ability to create material from the spiritual."

> **Read Genesis 1:1–3:**
> The Creation of the World
> **1** In the beginning, God created the heavens and the earth. ² The earth
> was without form and void, and darkness was over the face of the deep. And
> the Spirit of God was hovering over the face of the waters.
> ³ And God said, "Let there be light," and there was light.

First, we must understand the very nature of God's creation: He "spoke" it into existence from nothing (ex-nihilo). God is Spirit: invisible, omniscient, omnipresent, omnipotent. All authority emanates from Him, as He is and has the ultimate authority, which is the ability to create material from the spiritual. His creation is from His spoken Word.

> **Read John 1:1–3:**
> The Word Became Flesh: **1** In the beginning was the Word, and the Word was
> with God, and the Word was God. ² He was in the beginning with God. ³ All
> things were made through him, and without him was not any thing made that
> was made.

The spiritual trumps the material and is superior to the material; thus, the material is subordinate to the spiritual and under its authority. This is key for us to understand, as it explains why nothing is too difficult for Him; and why His power can change our circumstances, especially the adversity against us.

> **Read Genesis 1:26–27:**
> ²⁶ Then God said, "Let us make man[a] in our image, after our likeness. And let
> them have dominion over the fish of the sea and over the birds of the heavens
> and over the livestock and over all the earth and over every creeping thing that
> creeps on the earth."
>
> ²⁷ So God created man in his own image,
>     in the image of God he created him;
>     male and female he created them.

God created man in "Our" image. Who is "Our?" It is the Trinity—the Father, Son, and Holy Spirit are the triune God. One God, yet each distinct, and all the nature and characteristics of God are resident in all three. This includes authority. God originally gave this authority (dominion) over mankind to rule the Earth and be co-creators with Him in perfect communion with Him as created beings—with body (material), soul (seat of our personality, intellect, emotion, and will), and Spirit (His Spirit in us as ruler and leader of our lives). We were to live out this authority on Earth as we walked with Him and subdued the earth under the authority given us.

**2.** Exceptional Provision:

> **Read Genesis 1:28–30:**
>
> 28 And God blessed them. And God said to them, "Be fruitful and multiply and fill the earth and subdue it, and have dominion over the fish of the sea and over the birds of the heavens and over every living thing that moves on the earth." 29 And God said, "Behold, I have given you every plant yielding seed that is on the face of all the earth, and every tree with seed in its fruit. You shall have them for food. 30 And to every beast of the earth and to every bird of the heavens and to everything that creeps on the earth, everything that has the breath of life, I have given every green plant for food." And it was so.

God provided all that was needed to live and enjoy the fullness of His creation—all the plants, animals, and materials (organic and inorganic) were created so that we lacked nothing. It was all for our benefit to use, to build, and to make new things as we so were led through being co-creator with Him—and all this was subordinate to the spiritual. The word give means that He grants us, gives over to us, and delivers up to us all this exceptional provision. We would never be short of anything needed and were to enjoy abundance, so we would not have to be concerned about living conditions or making things work in this material world.

**3.** Exceptional Work:

> **Read Genesis 2:15:**
>
> [15] The Lord God took the man and put him in the garden of Eden to work it and keep it.

God gave to man and woman the assignment of "work," occupation and labor that served the purposes of God. They were to keep and care for this world through daily, meaningful occupation, which is simply defined as what we "do" every day to occupy our time in tasks for the benefit of progress and co-creating with God. Thus, this is not about earning income, but rather working at something we truly enjoy. So, a housewife who thoroughly enjoys taking care of children and the duties of being a wife is in an exceptional "occupation." We must understand that this is a part of God's nature that was given to mankind before the Fall; work is good and to be fulfilled by all of us. It brings much to us in the form of satisfaction, fulfillment, accomplishment, community with others, joy, and fun.

**4.** Exceptional Marriage and Relationship:

> **Read Genesis 2:18–25:**
>
> [18] Then the Lord God said, "It is not good that the man should be alone; I will make him a helper fit for[a] him." [19] Now out of the ground the Lord God had formed[b] every beast of the field and every bird of the heavens and brought them to the man to see what he would call them. And whatever the man called every living creature, that was its name. [20] The man gave names to all livestock and to the birds of the heavens and to every beast of the field. But for Adam[c] there was not found a helper fit for him. [21] So the Lord God caused a deep sleep to fall upon the man, and while he slept took one of his ribs and closed up its place with flesh. [22] And the rib that the Lord God had taken from the man he made[d] into a woman and brought her to the man. [23] Then the man said,

> "This at last is bone of my bones
>     and flesh of my flesh;
> she shall be called Woman,
>     because she was taken out of Man."[e]
> 24 Therefore a man shall leave his father and his mother and hold fast to his wife, and they shall become one flesh. 25 And the man and his wife were both naked and were not ashamed.

God said it is not good that man be alone, so He created "Wo-man" out of man, to be a helpmate, his counterpart in intimate relationship while living here on Earth. He said the two are to leave their father and mother. It is interesting that Adam and Eve had no mother and father. So, of what was He speaking? He was saying that all who were to come thereafter were to leave their upbringing behind and forge a new way together as a couple—to come together as one—living in unity and agreement. They were to live this way only with each other, as together they walked in the Spirit in complete unity with God, with the authority and dominion given to them as co-creators over Earth. As we live in unity in our exceptional marriage, it will be a place of blessing.

**Read Psalm 133:**

When Brothers Dwell in Unity
A Song of Ascents. Of David.
**133** Behold, how good and pleasant it is
    when brothers dwell in unity![a]
2 It is like the precious oil on the head,
    running down on the beard,
on the beard of Aaron,
    running down on the collar of his robes!
3 It is like the dew of Hermon,
    which falls on the mountains of Zion!
For there the Lord has commanded the blessing,
    life forevermore.

God states that it is good (most wonderful and favorable) and pleasant (delightful, lovely, fantastic) to dwell (live) in unity (united-ness, agreement, oneness). There He commands (orders, brings about with certainty) blessings—gifts of favor, prosperity, good things. So, through living in an exceptional marriage in unity, He promises His favor in life. Why would we not live there?

*Note: Think about God's original plan for mankind: Since we are physical, and thus, need to sleep for rest and recuperation, we were to get up to go to work and enjoy our exceptional occupation during the day; then, after work we were to go home and enjoy our exceptional marriage and family life.*

**Read Ecclesiastes 5:18–20; 9:9–10:**

18 Behold, what I have seen to be good and fitting is to eat and drink and find enjoyment[a] in all the toil with which one toils under the sun the few days of his life that God has given him, for this is his lot. 19 Everyone also to whom God has given wealth and possessions and power to enjoy them, and to accept his lot and rejoice in his toil—this is the gift of God. 20 For he will not much remember the days of his life because God keeps him occupied with joy in his heart.

9 Enjoy life with the wife whom you love, all the days of your vain[a] life that he has given you under the sun, because that is your portion in life and in your toil at which you toil under the sun. 10 Whatever your hand finds to do, do it with your might,[b] for there is no work or thought or knowledge or wisdom in Sheol, to which you are going.

God tells us there is nothing more important than enjoying our work and our marriage and family. It is to be the primary reason to rejoice and experience life to the full.

**5.** Exceptional Identity:

---

**Read Genesis 1:26; 1:31:**

[26] Then God said, "Let us make man[a] in our image, after our likeness. And let them have dominion over the fish of the sea and over the birds of the heavens and over the livestock and over all the earth and over every creeping thing that creeps on the earth."

[31] And God saw everything that he had made, and behold, it was very good. And there was evening and there was morning, the sixth day.

---

Adam and Eve understood that they were made in the likeness of God and were the children of the Most High God. They embraced their identity and lived fully in the bounty of the exceptional life provided by God. They did not reject it, diminish it, nor compromise on it. They lived like children of the King because they were! They were God's, and they knew it. This is reiterated in Song of Solomon 6:3: "I am my beloved's, and My beloved is mine." We are His loved ones, special and privileged to be His children.

**6.** Exceptional Health and Healing:

---

**Read Genesis: 1:26–2:25:**

[26] Then God said, "Let us make man[a] in our image, after our likeness. And let them have dominion over the fish of the sea and over the birds of the heavens and over the livestock and over all the earth and over every creeping thing that creeps on the earth."

[27] So God created man in his own image,
    in the image of God he created him;
      male and female he created them.

[28] And God blessed them. And God said to them, "Be fruitful and multiply and fill the earth and subdue it, and have dominion over the fish of the sea and over the birds of the heavens and over every living thing that moves on the

---

earth." 29 And God said, "Behold, I have given you every plant yielding seed that is on the face of all the earth, and every tree with seed in its fruit. You shall have them for food. 30 And to every beast of the earth and to every bird of the heavens and to everything that creeps on the earth, everything that has the breath of life, I have given every green plant for food." And it was so. 31 And God saw everything that he had made, and behold, it was very good. And there was evening and there was morning, the sixth day.

The Seventh Day, God Rests
**2** Thus the heavens and the earth were finished, and all the host of them. 2 And on the seventh day God finished his work that he had done, and he rested on the seventh day from all his work that he had done. 3 So God blessed the seventh day and made it holy, because on it God rested from all his work that he had done in creation.

The Creation of Man and Woman
4 These are the generations
of the heavens and the earth when they were created,
in the day that the Lord God made the earth and the heavens.

5 When no bush of the field[b] was yet in the land[c] and no small plant of the field had yet sprung up—for the Lord God had not caused it to rain on the land, and there was no man to work the ground, 6 and a mist[d] was going up from the land and was watering the whole face of the ground— 7 then the Lord God formed the man of dust from the ground and breathed into his nostrils the breath of life, and the man became a living creature. 8 And the Lord God planted a garden in Eden, in the east, and there he put the man whom he had formed. 9 And out of the ground the Lord God made to spring up every tree that is pleasant to the sight and good for food. The tree of life was in the midst of the garden, and the tree of the knowledge of good and evil.

10 A river flowed out of Eden to water the garden, and there it divided and became four rivers. 11 The name of the first is the Pishon. It is the one that flowed around the whole land of Havilah, where there is gold. 12 And the gold of that land is good; bdellium and onyx stone are there. 13 The name of the second river is the Gihon. It is the one that flowed around the whole land of Cush. 14 And the name of the third river is the Tigris, which flows east of Assyria. And the fourth river is the Euphrates.

> [15] The Lord God took the man and put him in the garden of Eden to work it and keep it. [16] And the Lord God commanded the man, saying, "You may surely eat of every tree of the garden, [17] but of the tree of the knowledge of good and evil you shall not eat, for in the day that you eat[e] of it you shall surely die." [18] Then the Lord God said, "It is not good that the man should be alone; I will make him a helper fit for[f] him." [19] Now out of the ground the Lord God had formed[g] every beast of the field and every bird of the heavens and brought them to the man to see what he would call them. And whatever the man called every living creature, that was its name. [20] The man gave names to all livestock and to the birds of the heavens and to every beast of the field. But for Adam[h] there was not found a helper fit for him. [21] So the Lord God caused a deep sleep to fall upon the man, and while he slept took one of his ribs and closed up its place with flesh. [22] And the rib that the Lord God had taken from the man he made[i] into a woman and brought her to the man. [23] Then the man said,
>
> "This at last is bone of my bones
>     and flesh of my flesh;
> she shall be called Woman,
>     because she was taken out of Man."[j]
>
> [24] Therefore a man shall leave his father and his mother and hold fast to his wife, and they shall become one flesh. [25] And the man and his wife were both naked and were not ashamed.

There was no sickness or illness in the Garden. God's exceptional life included health and healing. They lived in perfect health and enjoyed the beauty of not being concerned about physical issues.

**7.**  Exceptional Communion with Him:

In Genesis 1:26–2:25 (above), since Adam and Eve had body, soul, and Spirit, they had exceptional communion with God. They had regular communications, heard clearly what He had to say, could dialogue with Him at any time, and enjoyed their designed intimacy with Him all the time. They were His children, who lived in the beauty of a special relationship with the Almighty God, the creator of the universe, and had the confidence of knowing they were living in the exceptional life provided for and given by God.

**This is expressed further in John 10:3–5; 27–30:**

³ To him the gatekeeper opens. The sheep hear his voice, and he calls his own sheep by name and leads them out. ⁴ When he has brought out all his own, he goes before them, and the sheep follow him, for they know his voice. ⁵ A stranger they will not follow, but they will flee from him, for they do not know the voice of strangers."

²⁷ My sheep hear my voice, and I know them, and they follow me. ²⁸ I give them eternal life, and they will never perish, and no one will snatch them out of my hand. ²⁹ My Father, who has given them to me,[a] is greater than all, and no one is able to snatch them out of the Father's hand. ³⁰ I and the Father are one."

He is our Shepherd and knows us intimately, and we hear Him (attend to, consider what is or has been said; to understand, perceive the sense of what is said; to hear something; to perceive by the ear what is announced in one's presence), know Him (to see; to perceive with the eyes; to perceive by any of the senses; to perceive, notice, discern, discover) and follow Him (willingly go with Him where He leads us).

**He also describes this in John 15:1–8:**

I Am the True Vine
**15** "I am the true vine, and my Father is the vinedresser. ² Every branch in me that does not bear fruit he takes away, and every branch that does bear fruit he prunes, that it may bear more fruit. ³ Already you are clean because of the word that I have spoken to you. ⁴ Abide in me, and I in you. As the branch cannot bear fruit by itself, unless it abides in the vine, neither can you, unless you abide in me. ⁵ I am the vine; you are the branches. Whoever abides in me and I in him, he it is that bears much fruit, for apart from me you can do nothing. ⁶ If anyone does not abide in me he is thrown away like a branch and withers; and the branches are gathered, thrown into the fire, and burned. ⁷ If you abide in me, and my words abide in you, ask whatever you wish, and it will be done for you. ⁸ By this my Father is glorified, that you bear much fruit and so prove to be my disciples.

We are intimately connected to Him as the Branch to the Vine, with the Vinedresser (The Father) directing our lives through making our decisions. We remain in Him, and as a result, we bear fruit, more fruit, and much fruit. We glorify Him, as we abide in Him through our intimate relationship. Adam and Eve fully understood, "Apart from Him, we can do nothing." Why? Because of exceptional communion. How special is that!

Summary: In Genesis 1:31 it states: "Then God saw everything (all these exceptional characteristics of life with Him) that He had made, and indeed it was very good. So, the evening and the morning were the sixth day. The Earth was perfect. It had no destructive forces, no sin, no pain, no sickness, and no adversity. All was good—exceptionally and abundantly good! This Hebrew word is a very strong definition of what "good" means: pleasant, agreeable (to the senses); pleasant (to the higher nature), excellent, rich, valuable in estimation: glad, happy, prosperous. These seven exceptional qualities of God's creation before the Fall were amazingly, extraordinarily, supernaturally good. This was God's original plan—nothing but spectacular with no adversity—life abundant and life eternal. We must understand this as we look at the current state of the world with its common and normal adversity.

## A PROBLEM: THE FALL

**This wonderful life ended. In Genesis 3:1–13, we see what happened.**

The Fall

**3** Now the serpent was more crafty than any other beast of the field that the Lord God had made.

He said to the woman, "Did God actually say, 'You[a] shall not eat of any tree in the garden'?" 2 And the woman said to the serpent, "We may eat of the fruit of the trees in the garden, 3 but God said, 'You shall not eat of the fruit of the tree that is in the midst of the garden, neither shall you touch it, lest you die.'" 4 But the serpent said to the woman, "You will not surely die. 5 For God knows that when you eat of it your eyes will be opened, and you will be like God, knowing good and evil." 6 So when the woman saw that the tree was good for food, and that it was a delight to the eyes, and that the tree was to be desired to make one wise,[b] she took of its fruit and ate, and she also gave some to her husband who was with her, and he ate. 7 Then the eyes of both were opened, and they knew that they were naked. And they sewed fig leaves together and made themselves loincloths.

[8] And they heard the sound of the Lord God walking in the garden in the cool[c] of the day, and the man and his wife hid themselves from the presence of the Lord God among the trees of the garden. [9] But the Lord God called to the man and said to him, "Where are you?"[d] [10] And he said, "I heard the sound of you in the garden, and I was afraid, because I was naked, and I hid myself." [11] He said, "Who told you that you were naked? Have you eaten of the tree of which I commanded you not to eat?" [12] The man said, "The woman whom you gave to be with me, she gave me fruit of the tree, and I ate."[13] Then the Lord God said to the woman, "What is this that you have done?" The woman said, "The serpent deceived me, and I ate."

Satan had already been booted out of heaven. As Lucifer (an angel of light), he was number two in heaven with all the wonder and beauty of heaven; but decided with his free will to not choose God. God's creation of his higher beings—angels and man—include free will. True love is based upon free will—the ability to choose God or not.

**Read Isaiah 14:12–21:**

[12] "How you are fallen from heaven,
   O Day Star, son of Dawn!
How you are cut down to the ground,
   you who laid the nations low!
[13] You said in your heart,
   'I will ascend to heaven;
above the stars of God
   I will set my throne on high;
I will sit on the mount of assembly
   in the far reaches of the north;[a]
[14] I will ascend above the heights of the clouds;
   I will make myself like the Most High.'
[15] But you are brought down to Sheol,
   to the far reaches of the pit.
[16] Those who see you will stare at you
   and ponder over you:
'Is this the man who made the earth tremble,
   who shook kingdoms,

> <sup>17</sup> who made the world like a desert
>   and overthrew its cities,
>   who did not let his prisoners go home?'
> <sup>18</sup> All the kings of the nations lie in glory,
>   each in his own tomb;[b]
> <sup>19</sup> but you are cast out, away from your grave,
>   like a loathed branch,
> clothed with the slain, those pierced by the sword,
>   who go down to the stones of the pit,
>   like a dead body trampled underfoot.
> <sup>20</sup> You will not be joined with them in burial,
>   because you have destroyed your land,
>   you have slain your people.
> "May the offspring of evildoers
>   nevermore be named!
> <sup>21</sup> Prepare slaughter for his sons
>   because of the guilt of their fathers,
> lest they rise and possess the earth,
>   and fill the face of the world with cities."

In these verses we read that Lucifer wanted to be like God, so he made a move to take over. Not having the power of God (we must remember that Satan is not God—not omniscient, omnipresent, omnipotent—but a created being with limitations), he did not win this challenge to God (through this free will) and was consequently cast out of heaven. In addition, all the angels in heaven were given the opportunity to exercise their free will and were offered by God whom they wanted to follow. Two thirds of the angels chose to stay with and follow God (continuing to function as angelic heavenly hosts) and one third chose to leave and follow Satan (Rev. 12: 4). So, Satan and now his demons (fallen angels) had access to Earth and to Adam and Eve, but he had no authority to bring his destruction. So, what he had to do was appeal to Adam and Eve to exercise their free will and disobey God, so that Satan could receive the authority given to Adam and Eve (in Genesis 1:26 where this authority was given to mankind), and thereby, alter the nature of Earth to be dominated by Satan's nature of destruction. Satan appealed to Eve, and thus, to Adam who was right there with her to choose to eat of the forbidden tree (the tree of the Knowledge of Good and Evil in the middle of the garden). This tree was designated by God so that there was a real choice of exercising their free will, which included the free will to either choose God or not, as had Lucifer and the demonic angels. They had been warned by God that if they ate of this tree, they would surely die. Lucifer appealed to them that God surely did not say, "You would die," and then asked if they wanted to be like God.

As is true with our free will today, the real mistake that Adam and Eve made at this point was wondering about what God really did say, and exactly what it meant. Also, they did not go back to God with their open, perfect, and exceptional communion and ask God again to speak on this. They just drew their own conclusions, based upon the temptation of what they heard from Satan. As a result, they ate of the forbidden tree. At that moment they did die, as spoken by God. What actually died? Man and woman were created as body (real material), soul (the seat of intellect, personality, emotion, and will) and spirit (God's Holy Spirit). Animals are just body and soul and driven by instincts (self- preservation). So, at the Fall, the spirit of man and woman died. The Holy Spirit had to vacate. They became a very sophisticated, intellectually superior animal now, driven by instinct and self-centeredness. Their nature changed. It became a sin nature devoid of the Spirit of God and no longer holy. This impeded their ability to have direct relationship with God, because He is holy and requires perfection. Thus, the nature of the world changed. It went from the beauty, perfection, and all the exceptional goodness of God and His original creation to the nature of Satan.

> **Read John 10:10:**
>
> [10] The thief comes only to steal and kill and destroy. I came that they may have life and have it abundantly.

This verse tells us that Satan seeks to steal, kill, and destroy. It must be noted that the only remedy is to be "born again," to have the Spirit re-enter our nature and give us the ability to receive Christ's life in us. But at the Fall, everything on Earth (both animate and inanimate) went to and is still operating in destruction, which is called entropy. This includes all things, like steel bridges that collapse in Minneapolis, like the coliseum in Rome, etc. So, everything left alone will go to destruction, and this destructive world is being led by those in power who are fallen, sinful people who operate purely selfishly. It should not surprise us, then, that the world is literally going to "hell in a hand basket" and getting more and more wicked, full of the values of anti-God. When Adam and Eve exercised their free will and disobeyed God's will, they thwarted the original plan of exceptional life in an exceptional creation and handed over the authority and sinful nature of man and the world destruction to Satan. The world is now a place of great trouble, great adversity, and great difficulty. This has become normal and is getting even more so.

The enemy's world in which we live is shown in John 10:10, which reveals the essence of the enemy. He aims to steal (take away by theft, i.e., take away by stealth); kill (put to death good things); and destroy (to put out of the way entirely, abolish, put an end to ruin, render useless). It is relentless and never ending. There is no breather. Our world is the world of the enemy, so naturally, it is a place where things oppose us and where things are not intended to go well for us. This is so that we do not seek God and learn to abide and remain in Him, but to rather blame God for these awful things that happen to us.

> **1.    Luke 4:5–8:**
>
> [5] And the devil took him up and showed him all the kingdoms of the world in a moment of time, [6] and said to him, "To you I will give all this authority and their glory, for it has been delivered to me, and I give it to whom I will. [7] If you, then, will worship me, it will all be yours." [8] And Jesus answered him, "It is written,
> "'You shall worship the Lord your God,
>       and him only shall you serve.'"

Satan tempts Christ by offering the kingdoms of the world to Him. He can accept this offer and then take back the authority without having to go to the cross. The intent is for Christ to just subordinate Himself to Satan. This was a real temptation, which meant that Satan actually had the ability to deliver the kingdom of the world (which was now his since it was given to him by Adam and Eve). The Greek word, "kingdom" here means power, kingship, dominion, rule, the right or authority to rule over a kingdom. "Power" is another word for authority and dominion. If it was not real, Christ would have dismissed it knowing that it was not Satan's to give, so nothing real was  being offered. Rather, Christ said, "Yes, you do have this authority now," but He still chooses not to take a shortcut but only worship and follow the Father. His will was to choose God.

Note a very profound truth: Adam and Eve exercised self-will and fell into sin. The only way to restore this nature of sin now within all mankind born into the world from Adam and Eve was for God Himself (Christ) to exercise His self-will and not succumb to these temptations at the beginning of His ministry on Earth. He then needed to exercise His self-will in Gethsemane on His way to the cross at the end of His ministry, so that based upon His free will, it was purely His choice, as read in John 10:17–18:

> [17] For this reason the Father loves me, because I lay down my life that I may take it up again. [18] No one takes it from me, but I lay it down of my own accord. I have authority to lay it down, and I have authority to take it up again. This charge I have received from my Father."

He marched to the cross where the sin was placed upon Him and satisfied the Father's requirement of perfection (propitiation/sacrifice). He obtained back the authority for man to once again be "born again" through belief. This enabled us to have the Holy Spirit restored in our nature. Christ did acknowledge that Satan had the authority of worldly kingdoms operating on earth and that the nature of his kingdoms was destruction: to steal, kill, and destroy.

> **2.  1 John 5:18–20:**
>
> [18] We know that everyone who has been born of God does not keep on sinning, but he who was born of God protects him, and the evil one does not touch him. [19] We know that we are from God, and the whole world lies in the power of the evil one.
>
> [20] And we know that the Son of God has come and has given us understanding, so that we may know him who is true; and we are in him who is true, in his Son Jesus Christ. He is the true God and eternal life.

John wrote 60 years after the resurrection that Satan still had control over this world. Though Christ has taken back the authority, His authority operates in His Kingdom, which now is available to us to live in; but we also live in the natural world that is still under the authority of Satan (which is what we would call enemy territory). The Greek word here for wickedness means full of labor, annoyances, hardships, pressed and harassed, toil, full of peril, pain and trouble, evil, wicked, and bad. That pretty well describes our world. It should not surprise us that this characterizes everyday life. Though believers, we live in enemy territory and are subject to this normal wickedness. As believers we are called to live in both kingdoms—within the Kingdom of God which is righteousness, peace, and joy in the Holy Spirit—while we also traverse through enemy territory in a world under the control of the enemy. This world is still characterized by destruction: steal, kill, and destroy.

> **Read Romans 14:17:**
>
> [17] For the kingdom of God is not a matter of eating and drinking but of righteousness and peace and joy in the Holy Spirit.

We must fully understand that though Satan has been defeated by Christ, and all authority has now been given to Christ, this is spiritual authority, which does trump temporal authority. However, this is only appropriated by believers who are walking in the Spirit in His Kingdom. We exist within these two kingdoms. The worldly kingdom is still the nature of entropy with dark principalities and powers still operating. We are not exempt from this kingdom, and adversity will still occur in our everyday lives.

The Fall happened, and man received a self-centered sin nature, with which all are born. The world went from being perfect with exceptional living to one of difficulty, adversity, and wickedness as the norm. We cannot escape it and are all subject to it.

## THE FATHER HAS ANOTHER PLAN TO RESTORE THE ORIGINAL PLAN: CHRIST, OUR REDEEMER, OUR RESTORER.

Though the world has been lost to destruction under the control of the enemy, and our nature is now a sin nature dominated by self, the Father has provided another plan. He has given us a Redeemer who can bring us again back to the beautiful, restored life intended by God. Salvation and being born again is not just a ticket to heaven, but it is an invitation to a restoration of the original, exceptional life intended by God in the Garden of Eden. Christ has come to bring us this exceptional life now.

> **1.  John 10:10:**
>
> [17] For the kingdom of God is not a matter of eating and drinking but of righteousness and peace and joy in the Holy Spirit.

The words spoken by Christ here are the same words used by the Father in Genesis 1:31: This life that Christ has come to give us is the exceptional, super-abundant, good life intended in the Garden of Eden. His death and resurrection conquered death and Satan, and thus, we do not have to live under the control and influence of the destructive enemy. Rather, we can reverse the destruction and receive to the point of possessing and owning this super-abundant (exceedingly, supremely, extraordinary, more remarkable, more excellent) life. This life is the full, genuine, real, active, vigorous, fullness of life of God. This is to be lived out in this destructive world, as we live in the Kingdom of God, in the Spirit, and in Christ. It is not just for heaven but for the now. Thus, while we will have adversity since we live in enemy territory, we have this exceptional, abundant life offered to us.

2.    Luke 4:16–21; Isaiah 61:

Jesus Rejected at Nazareth

[16] And he came to Nazareth, where he had been brought up. And as was his custom, he went to the synagogue on the Sabbath day, and he stood up to read. [17] And the scroll of the prophet Isaiah was given to him. He unrolled the scroll and found the place where it was written,

[18] "The Spirit of the Lord is upon me,
    because he has anointed me
    to proclaim good news to the poor.
He has sent me to proclaim liberty to the captives
    and recovering of sight to the blind,
    to set at liberty those who are oppressed,
[19] to proclaim the year of the Lord's favor."
[20] And he rolled up the scroll and gave it back to the attendant and sat down. And the eyes of all in the synagogue were fixed on him. [21] And he began to say to them, "Today this Scripture has been fulfilled in your hearing."

The Year of the Lord's Favor

**61** The Spirit of the Lord God is upon me,
    because the Lord has anointed me
to bring good news to the poor;[a]
    he has sent me to bind up the brokenhearted,
to proclaim liberty to the captives,
    and the opening of the prison to those who are bound;[b]
[2] to proclaim the year of the Lord's favor,
    and the day of vengeance of our God;
    to comfort all who mourn;
[3] to grant to those who mourn in Zion—
    to give them a beautiful headdress instead of ashes,

the oil of gladness instead of mourning,
  the garment of praise instead of a faint spirit;
that they may be called oaks of righteousness,
  the planting of the Lord, that he may be glorified.[c]
4 They shall build up the ancient ruins;
  they shall raise up the former devastations;
they shall repair the ruined cities,
  the devastations of many generations.
5 Strangers shall stand and tend your flocks;
  foreigners shall be your plowmen and vinedressers;
6 but you shall be called the priests of the Lord;
  they shall speak of you as the ministers of our God;
you shall eat the wealth of the nations,
  and in their glory you shall boast.
7 Instead of your shame there shall be a double portion;
  instead of dishonor they shall rejoice in their lot;
therefore in their land they shall possess a double portion;
  they shall have everlasting joy.
8 For I the Lord love justice;
  I hate robbery and wrong;[d]
I will faithfully give them their recompense,
  and I will make an everlasting covenant with them.
9 Their offspring shall be known among the nations,
  and their descendants in the midst of the peoples;
all who see them shall acknowledge them,
  that they are an offspring the Lord has blessed.
10 I will greatly rejoice in the Lord;
  my soul shall exult in my God,
for he has clothed me with the garments of salvation;
  he has covered me with the robe of righteousness,
as a bridegroom decks himself like a priest with a beautiful headdress,
  and as a bride adorns herself with her jewels.
11 For as the earth brings forth its sprouts,
  and as a garden causes what is sown in it to sprout up,
so the Lord God will cause righteousness and praise
  to sprout up before all the nations.

Luke 4 describes the first public statement of Christ about His ministry. He goes to the synagogue in Nazareth, which He had been to many times since He lived there, and is handed the Scroll of Isaiah 61 to read. He reads it and states publicly (after sitting down to make an emphatic point) that Isaiah 61 has been fulfilled in Him, and He has come to bring this redemptive, beautiful life to us now and not just a ticket to heaven. This beautiful life includes healing up our wounds (to bind up, repair). We are all wounded and have patterns in our lives that are destructive and cause us difficulty. Christ promises to heal us so that these wounds are fully restored to health, and thus, no longer cause us difficulty or lead us to our poor responses to things in life. Instead, they give us liberty (free-flowing freedom) and free us up from being captive. All of us are captive to certain patterns and ways of how we look at and respond to life. We can be living in un-forgiveness, full of anger, always frustrated, responding in fear, worry, and anxiety, etc., and no matter how much we try, we cannot seem to live in freedom, and thus, we remain in our captivity. Christ promises us that He will lead us to freedom and release us from our patterns of captivity so that our life is full of joy and wonder. Christ gives us comfort (brings compassion, console, hope) when we are downtrodden, burdened, grieving, and disappointed, because the situations in our lives are not working well or not what we thought they would be. We have a tendency to go to resignation and accept that this life is troublesome, is never going to be great (perhaps once in a while but certainly not as the norm), and something we just have to put up with it. Christ promises that He will give us comfort and show us how wonderful life can be as we walk with Him.

He also promises that He can make beauty (ornaments, value) from ashes. Throughout our life, we often ruin or have ruined things that literally are ashes (of no value and no hope of amounting to anything). Christ has such amazing supernatural power that He can bring worthless, dead things back to life, back to value, and back to such beauty that it is exceptional (i.e., the original exceptional life of Genesis). He can deliver joy and praise from things that have not gone well and are heavy and weighing on us. Instead of going to worry, fear, and anxiety, He causes us to experience true joy and praise to the extent that we are thrilled at the life He has brought and the hope of the promises ahead, even if we are currently experiencing difficulty.

Further, He promises to build up and repair from our ruins (construct, rebuild, re-establish to original, make new again). Isn't this wonderful? What we have ruined through our sin and terrible choices can all be restored to God's original plan, and it matters not how much it is ruined. This is the Good News. He can redeem and restore anything! He can take what has been ruined by the enemy (stolen, killed, and destroyed) or by us through not following Him, and He can make it beautiful, restored, or rebuilt. This sums up the wonderful ministry of Christ today. It's not just a ticket to heaven, but it has come to give us the abundant, exceptional life now that He has uniquely planned for us. Remember, He is not a respecter of persons, with some being lucky and others not. He has come and offers exceptional life to all who are His children.

The people of the world now have a clear choice. We can continue to live as self-centered people in a fallen world that is self-destructing, or we can live as a child of God who is redeemed. Then the children of God have two choices to make: (1) to live in His kingdom through abiding in Him ("Apart from Him we can do nothing" – John 15:5), walking in the Spirit, and thus, experiencing the restoration of the exceptional life ("I have come to give you life and give it super abundantly" – John 10:10); or (2) live a carnal life in the flesh (remain self-centered) and again put to death the Spirit (still resident in us, but operating as if not there), be at enmity against God's will (live outside His Kingdom life), and not able to please Him (Romans 8:5–8). As we will see in Section 2, by living in the Kingdom and abiding and walking in the Spirit, we cannot avoid all adversity. There are certain adversities that are brought purposely by God to cause us to repent and turn away from our carnal living as a believer, so these adversities will be experienced, though they need not be.

For the unbeliever there is a deepening sense of adversity that characterizes their life on a global and national level, as well as on a personal level. There is judgment against mankind on a global, national, local, and personal level, because the truth stands, regardless of whether we seek it or understand it; and there really is no excuse, since there is built within us a sense that there is something greater than us. There are plenty of physical indicators available to all who can see that there is something greater than us. Romans 1:18 and 2:16 explain this in great detail. The wrath (judgment of God) is revealed against all ungodliness, for God has revealed Himself to all, and thus, none are without excuse. They are living futile lives and are foolishly thinking they are wise having exchanged the glory of the incorruptible God for the corruptible idols of man. Because of this, God gives them over to their sad, adversity-filled lives and their evil passions (like homosexuality, greed, adultery, strife, deceit, etc.) that only promote more adversity. Those who are self-seeking and do not seek nor follow the truth, but rather pursue unrighteousness which they have believed to be righteous, will experience indignation, wrath, tribulation, and anguish. In other words, they receive major adversity as normal. If we step from our own time back in history and look at all of history visiting each era and observing, we would basically see awful, difficult things and great adversity all over the place. Regardless of our station in life, none of us would want to go back to another time if we really knew what it was like. We Americans have been blessed, because we were a nation under God and received blessings of prosperity, standard of living, freedom, avoidance of war on our soil (except civil war between ourselves), and the expectation and hope that things would always get better. Thus, our level of general adversity (see description in Chapter 4) has been relatively protected and contained, because we were a nation under God.

Today, I believe that is not so, and we are suffering the consequences of Romans 1 and 2 as a nation. God is giving over our nation to its uncleanness and vile passions, withdrawing His protection over adversity and actually bringing about His promised indignation, wrath, tribulation, and anguish. It is going to get worse, and those of us who are still living in the Kingdom of God are not exempt from this global and national scale of adversity, which characterizes most of history on earth. Our lives are going to become more difficult, frustrating, and painful, not because our government and rulers cannot quite get it right regardless of political persuasion, but because we are dealing in spiritual things and live outside of God's protection, it will typically be full of adversity. This should not surprise us, nor should we think that we are exempt.

### SUMMARY of LESSON 1:

- God originally planned an exceptional life for His creation, mankind:

  - Exceptional Authority
  - Exceptional Provision
  - Exceptional Work
  - Exceptional Marriage
  - Exceptional Identity
  - Exceptional Health and Healing
  - Exceptional Communion with God

Adam and Eve fully enjoyed this life in the Garden of Eden. It was theirs to enjoy, and it truly was exceptional. This life is a picture for us to see as His original plan; a plan though lost through the Fall of man, is still available to us today.

- Satan came and tempted Adam and Eve by appealing to them to exercise their self-will by disobeying God and His instruction to not eat of the tree of the Knowledge of Good and Evil; and that if they did, they would surely die. They did go to "self" and ate of the tree, and surely did die. They lost the Spirit that was resident in them. They handed over to Satan the authority of the Earth that had been given to them by God; and as a result, Satan gained control over the world with an operation of destruction—steal, kill, and destroy—which is entropy, where everything is going to decay, and finally, destruction. So, with sinful, selfish mankind living on Earth and operating as a sophisticated animal with self-centered decisions and the Earth becoming a place of destruction, our life is going to experience trouble, tribulation, difficulty, annoyance, hardship, oppression, bad things happening, adversity. It is now normal, and until Christ returns, is also irreversible. We live in enemy territory and cannot escape the difficult place we live in.

- God provided another way. He brought His new Kingdom where He can restore His original plan—the exceptional life—to those who believe and walk in what He has provided. Through Christ's redemptive work at the cross, where He took the penalty for the deserved punishment for sin, we were given back the authority that was lost by mankind to Satan. Those who believe (and are born again and have the Spirit reenter their life) now have the opportunity to overcome the destructive world we live in and have Christ restore to us His original plan of the exceptional, abundant life. Thus, we live in two kingdoms—the Kingdom of God, which is superior in power and might; and the kingdom of Earth that is still controlled by Satan with the nature of destruction and entropy. As believers, we have the choice to "walk in the Spirit" and operate in His Kingdom, under His rulership, leading and guiding, and under His supernatural work in, through, and around us; or, we can live in the carnal (self) and leave the Kingdom life and be subject to the kingdom of the world and all its destruction—and will surely experience adversity. It is our choice (Deuteronomy 30:11–20): We can choose Him and walk in the Kingdom where there is life and blessing; or by not choosing Him and not walking in the Kingdom, we experience death and curses. Since we live in the two kingdoms with its exceptional life of God, in the middle of enemy territory with its destructive forces, we are to understand that adversity is always present. It should not surprise us that adversity will impact our lives, even as we are living in the Kingdom and experiencing His exceptional life for us.

The key is to understand the nature of adversity, the different causes of adversity, and then our responses to the adversity in these different scenarios.

# LESSON 2:
## TYPES AND CAUSES OF REAL ADVERSITY

Let's look at the typical types of adversity that we face in our lives:

1. Frustration – This comes when things are not going well, things are not working, there are delays, traffic, red lights, delivery did not come on time, order that came was incorrect, things break down (particularly when needed – i.e., the air conditioner on a hot day).

   Satan wants to make frustration and move us out of the Kingdom. This causes us so to lose our peace, joy, freedom, and perhaps then moves us to selfishness where we lose protection and onto a path of his direct attack.

2. Life Difficulties – The severity of these determine our reaction to and our level of anxiety. Perhaps we have financial reversal (stock market bottoms out to a position that we were not expecting; an asset we own, like a boat, house, or rental property, has an unexpected financial loss, a renter doesn't pay for damages made to a property), a car accident (particularly if not our fault), a business issue (customer loss or major complaint, or major service issue, employee loss, complaint, or lawsuit, poor performance by employees, vendor loss, new government law or lawsuit, new costs, inability to pass on costs to customer through price increases, drop in margin, change in technology, economic model changing, cash flow issues, market changes, or you're feeling tired and weary and stuck; no margin), or working too much, or government actions that change our way of life (like COVID-19 with quarantines, economic shutdown, limited freedom to operate, wearing masks, limited social gatherings for sports, concerts, church worship, etc.).

3. Relationship Issues – If your marriage is not doing well, you are angry at each other, arguing much of the time, or have other family issues, or the kids are not doing well because they've made poor choices and are suffering with their consequences, and while you feel bad for them and are trying to help, but find you are not really helping. Or, you find that parents and siblings are operating in

dysfunctional ways and affecting your family and you; church has similar dysfunctional issues that affect you, especially if in a leadership role. Or maybe you have friends who are causing problems; or maybe you have opposition from specific individuals in business, ministry, community groups and are against you and what you believe to be the will and promises of God either directly or indirectly. And, to you, things not only lack progression, but even seem to be sliding backward.

4. Health Issues – Are you experiencing physical problems? The range of issues includes colds/flus that last awhile that are just nuisances to severe accidents to long-term disabilities to long-term, life-ending diagnoses, such as cancer. We can go from enjoying a normal physical life to all of a sudden living a life consumed by the physical condition that needs a resolution because it is limiting our ability to function normally, even temporarily as with the cold/flu. One of the enemy's techniques is to get us to accept this as "God's will" so we now spend the rest of our life or a period of our life hampered and less than best and limited in living the abundant life. God uses the physical to get our attention about something spiritual going on, since it is so critical to our well-being and we cannot ignore it.

5. Surprises – In any of the above categories and those we cannot even imagine, something can happen beyond our control, out of the blue, suddenly. It can even be global (a war starts, the stock market declines, and we lose big), a new law is passed, a new competitor enters the market (Uber into the taxi market), someone in our world decides to go after us, our company, or you personally, etc., and it changes our world as we must now focus on this new adversity.

**WHAT KIND OF ADVERSITIES ARE YOU ENCOUNTERING RIGHT NOW? DESCRIBE IN DETAIL AND THE EFFECT THEY ARE HAVING AT THE MOMENT.**

_______________________________________________________________

_______________________________________________________________

_______________________________________________________________

_______________________________________________________________

_______________________________________________________________

_______________________________________________________________

_______________________________________________________________

## CAUSES OF ADVERSITY

### GENERAL ADVERSITY

What will we experience? Why?

What does Jesus tell us about what will happen to us in this world? Why? What does this mean for our everyday lives?

> **Read John 16:33:**
>
> [33] I have said these things to you, that in me you may have peace. In the world you will have tribulation. But take heart; I have overcome the world."

_______________________________________________

_______________________________________________

_______________________________________________

_______________________________________________

_______________________________________________

> **Remember John 10:10:**
>
> [10] The thief comes only to steal and kill and destroy. I came that they may have life and have it abundantly.

_______________________________________________

_______________________________________________

_______________________________________________

_______________________________________________

_______________________________________________

**Read Psalm 107:23–28:**

23 Some went down to the sea in ships,
   doing business on the great waters;
24 they saw the deeds of the Lord,
   his wondrous works in the deep.
25 For he commanded and raised the stormy wind,
   which lifted up the waves of the sea.
26 They mounted up to heaven; they went down to the depths;
   their courage melted away in their evil plight;
27 they reeled and staggered like drunken men
   and were at their wits' end.[a]
28 Then they cried to the Lord in their trouble,
   and he delivered them from their distress.

_________________________________________________

_________________________________________________

_________________________________________________

_________________________________________________

_________________________________________________

_________________________________________________

If the mountains are shaking, what does that mean for us? How should we react to this?

**Read Psalm 46:1–7:**

God Is Our Fortress
To the choirmaster. Of the Sons of Korah. According to Alamoth.[a] A Song.
**46** God is our refuge and strength,
   a very present[b] help in trouble.
2 Therefore we will not fear though the earth gives way,
   though the mountains be moved into the heart of the sea,
3 though its waters roar and foam,
   though the mountains tremble at its swelling. Selah

> 4 There is a river whose streams make glad the city of God,
>   the holy habitation of the Most High.
> 5 God is in the midst of her; she shall not be moved;
>   God will help her when morning dawns.
> 6 The nations rage, the kingdoms totter;
>   he utters his voice, the earth melts.
> 7 The Lord of hosts is with us;
>   the God of Jacob is our fortress. Selah

---
---
---
---
---

What is trouble? How does it affect us, and how do we react to it?

> **Read Psalm 91:14–16:**
>
> 14 "Because he holds fast to me in love, I will deliver him;
>   I will protect him, because he knows my name.
> 15 When he calls to me, I will answer him;
>   I will be with him in trouble;
>   I will rescue him and honor him.
> 16 With long life I will satisfy him
>   and show him my salvation."

---
---
---
---
---

**TEST OF FAITH**

What does God say about this type of trial? What is it for? Why?

> **Read James 1:2–5:**
>
> Testing of Your Faith
> 2 Count it all joy, my brothers,[a] when you meet trials of various kinds, 3 for you know that the testing of your faith produces steadfastness. 4 And let steadfastness have its full effect, that you may be perfect and complete, lacking in nothing.
>
> 5 If any of you lacks wisdom, let him ask God, who gives generously to all without reproach, and it will be given him.

_______________________________________

_______________________________________

_______________________________________

_______________________________________

_______________________________________

What is the purpose of these trials? What is God doing for us in these? Why?

> **Read 1 Peter 1:3–9:**
>
> Born Again to a Living Hope
> 3 Blessed be the God and Father of our Lord Jesus Christ! According to his great mercy, he has caused us to be born again to a living hope through the resurrection of Jesus Christ from the dead, 4 to an inheritance that is imperishable, undefiled, and unfading, kept in heaven for you, 5 who by God's power are being guarded through faith for a salvation ready to be revealed in the last time. 6 In this you rejoice, though now for a little while, if necessary, you have been grieved by various trials, 7 so that the tested genuineness of your faith—more precious than gold that perishes though it is tested by fire—may be found to result in praise and glory and honor at the revelation of Jesus Christ. 8 Though you have not seen him, you love him. Though you do not now

> see him, you believe in him and rejoice with joy that is inexpressible and filled with glory,[9] obtaining the outcome of your faith, the salvation of your souls.

_______________________________________________

_______________________________________________

_______________________________________________

_______________________________________________

_______________________________________________

What do these verses speak about faith? What is important to understand about the definition of faith? Why?

**Read Hebrews 11:1–3:**

By Faith
**11** Now faith is the assurance of things hoped for, the conviction of things not seen. [2] For by it the people of old received their commendation. [3] By faith we understand that the universe was created by the word of God, so that what is seen was not made out of things that are visible.

_______________________________________________

_______________________________________________

_______________________________________________

_______________________________________________

_______________________________________________

What must we understand about the importance of faith? Why? What is to be our role in receiving faith?

**Read Hebrews 11:6:**

[6] And without faith it is impossible to please him, for whoever would draw near to God must believe that he exists and that he rewards those who seek him.

_______________________________________________

_______________________________________________

_______________________________________________

_______________________________________________

_______________________________________________

What does this say about Christ's role in giving us faith? What does this practically mean?

> **Read Hebrews 12:1–2:**
>
> Jesus, Founder and Perfecter of Our Faith
> **12** Therefore, since we are surrounded by so great a cloud of witnesses, let us also lay aside every weight, and sin which clings so closely, and let us run with endurance the race that is set before us, [2] looking to Jesus, the founder and perfecter of our faith, who for the joy that was set before him endured the cross, despising the shame, and is seated at the right hand of the throne of God.

_______________________________________________

_______________________________________________

_______________________________________________

_______________________________________________

How do we receive and process faith? How is this done practically?

> **Read Romans 10:17:**
>
> [17] So faith comes from hearing, and hearing through the word of Christ.

___________________________________________

___________________________________________

___________________________________________

___________________________________________

___________________________________________

As He gives us faith—finishes our faith—the Biblical truth is that faith comes from hearing what He says—hearing from the Word of God. So, as you listen to His promises, your role is to diligently seek Him, stay in the Word until they, His promises, become certain. Do you have certainty?

**The two issues are:**

1.  Do you even care? Do you wish to go to Him for Him to author faith? Most people don't. That's why they never get anywhere. They're always frustrated, and they're always experiencing adversity because they don't even care to hear what God has to say. And God saying, well, you're wandering around with all this adversity, and you don't even care what I have to say to resolve it. And there's nothing I can do other than to let you experience all these different causes of adversity. And you don't even know what's going on other than that you are experiencing pain, difficulty, and stress. And you're digging yourself deeper and deeper and deeper into holes. You ultimately fight each other, divorce each other, cause conflict, makes stupid mistakes, get yourself in more trouble and have more problems, etc.

2.  You blame God when something doesn't come to pass. You are not willing to let Him finish taking you to faith, to certainty. You heard what He had to say, but when you fail the test of faith, when the circumstances go south, you go back to doubt and trying to resolve it on your own. You've heard it, and you've been processing it in the Word. And you come to a point where you think, you know what, I think I believe this. And He's going to say, well, let's go prove it out in the circumstances that have or will go south on you. Now, is it to punish you? No. Is it to beat you up? No. It's only to prove it out, to determine if you believe with certainty. Will you fail the test? If you fail the test, you go back to worry, anxiety, or, oh my gosh, it isn't going to happen because I don't really believe this. He reminds us to stay with Him because He hasn't finished rewarding you with faith. You may think you are finished or that He is showing us that we are finished, but we are not. The worst thing you can do is think you're finished and then quit. It is for this reason that He has given us this test of faith. The testing is to reveal that we must continue to stay with Him so that He can finish taking us to certainty and giving us faith to believe. It is then that He can fulfill what He has spoken.

Example of testing: Abraham:

In these two sets of verses, what does it reveal about the faith of Abraham? Based upon Abraham's life, what do we know about his struggle with faith? What did he do well and no so well? Why is this so important in our life of faith?

**Read Romans 4:17–21:**

[17] as it is written, "I have made you the father of many nations"—in the presence of the God in whom he believed, who gives life to the dead and calls into existence the things that do not exist. [18] In hope he believed against hope, that he should become the father of many nations, as he had been told, "So shall your offspring be." [19] He did not weaken in faith when he considered his own body, which was as good as dead (since he was about a hundred years old), or when he considered the barrenness[a] of Sarah's womb. [20] No unbelief made him waver concerning the promise of God, but he grew strong in his faith as he gave glory to God, [21] fully convinced that God was able to do what he had promised.

---
---
---
---
---

**Read Genesis 22:1–18:**

The Sacrifice of Isaac

**22** After these things God tested Abraham and said to him, "Abraham!" And he said, "Here I am." [2] He said, "Take your son, your only son Isaac, whom you love, and go to the land of Moriah, and offer him there as a burnt offering on one of the mountains of which I shall tell you." [3] So Abraham rose early in the morning, saddled his donkey, and took two of his young men with him, and his son Isaac. And he cut the wood for the burnt offering and arose and went to the place of which God had told him. [4] On the third day Abraham lifted up his eyes and saw the place from afar. [5] Then Abraham said to his young men, "Stay here with the donkey; I and the boy[a] will go over there and worship and come again to you."[6] And Abraham took the wood of the burnt offering and laid it on Isaac his son. And he took in his hand the fire and the knife. So they went both of them together. [7] And Isaac said to his father Abraham, "My father!" And he said, "Here I am, my son." He said, "Behold, the fire and the wood, but where is the lamb for a burnt offering?" [8] Abraham said, "God will provide for himself the lamb for a burnt offering, my son." So they went both of them together.

[9] When they came to the place of which God had told him, Abraham built the altar there and laid the wood in order and bound Isaac his son and laid him on the altar, on top of the wood. [10] Then Abraham reached out his hand and took the knife to slaughter his son. [11] But the angel of the Lord called to him from heaven and said, "Abraham, Abraham!" And he said, "Here I am." [12] He said, "Do not lay your hand on the boy or do anything to him, for now I know that you fear God, seeing you have not withheld your son, your only son, from me." [13] And Abraham lifted up his eyes and looked, and behold, behind him was a ram, caught in a thicket by his horns. And Abraham went and took the ram and offered it up as a burnt offering instead of his son. [14] So Abraham called the name of that place, "The Lord will provide";[b] as it is said to this day, "On the mount of the Lord it shall be provided."[c]

[15] And the angel of the Lord called to Abraham a second time from heaven[16] and said, "By myself I have sworn, declares the Lord, because you have done this and have not withheld your son, your only son, [17] I will surely bless you, and I will surely multiply your offspring as the stars of heaven and as the sand that is on the seashore. And your offspring shall possess the gate of his[d] enemies,[18] and in your offspring shall all the nations of the earth be blessed, because you have obeyed my voice."

_______________________________________________

_______________________________________________

_______________________________________________

_______________________________________________

_______________________________________________

# LESSON 3:
## CAUSES OF ADVERSITY (CONTINUED)

## PRUNING

This is entirely God's work; and is intended to cut back our activities and involvements, so that His desired fruit is produced. We, by becoming too involved and burdened by too many things to do, wind up having little or no fruit. Thus, God will bring adversity in what we are doing, so that we realize we are doing too much; and need to let him rearrange our life and create space and margin for us to receive the needed sunlight (the Son) and the needed water (the Holy Spirit) to enjoy being a branch and producing much (but not too much) high-quality fruit.

1.  PRUNING (CUTTING BACK GROWTH OF THE BRANCH THAT IS GETTING TOO BIG TO PRODUCE FRUIT):

    a.  Only healthy branches that are capable of bearing fruit are pruned. Unless pruned properly, pruning can actually cause the branch to die and have to be discarded; and only the vinedresser knows how to do it. Each branch is individual, so there is no one system for all branches. If pruned too much or too little, there will be no fruit. It has to be exactly what is needed for that particular branch. To protect from expected adversity (less than normal rain, potential frost, heat, wind, etc.), the location of the pruning is exact, so as to allow the branch to survive the adversity. Again, only the vinedresser knows this, and if not done properly, this incorrect pruning will result in the branch dying, not because of too little or too much, but because it's done in the wrong location.

    Key Revelation: Only the Vinedresser (the Father) knows exactly how much and where to prune. If we try to do this ourselves; or allow others to do this who are not the Vinedresser (churches, pastors, advisors, friends, spouses, etc.), we will make mistakes and actually accelerate our becoming useless and bearing no fruit.

b. The pruning has to be such that the branches and the leaves that will come and be continually pruned must have plenty of sun (SON) and water (HOLY SPIRIT) to be able to thrive. If after the initial pruning it starts to get too big (crowding as it flourishes, particularly in the center of the vine), it blocks the sunlight and water from the branches. Then as they get too big (although they are actually very healthy), the overgrowth then diminishes their ability to receive what is needed to thrive, and they shrink and then do not produce fruit.

c. After the initial pruning, the branches grow "shoots" from which the grapes ultimately are created and grow in bunches. As these shoots begin to grow, the vinedresser prunes the shoots right away (just after they pop out) so that there is plenty of space for the sunlight and water. The pruning, both initially and as the branch grows itself and sprouts shoots, is required to provide plenty of open space for the sunlight and rain to reach the branches, the leaves, and soak into the dirt that is necessary for strength of the vine.

Key Revelation: Pruning is ongoing and is geared to create space for sunlight and water, which are the sources of life. This is in addition to the primary reason of having the branch not get so big that the sap can't get through the branch into the fruit and so that water (Holy Spirit) is not absorbed by the branch resulting in no fruit. The Covenant: Blessed to become a blessing by giving it away. Our abiding is to fully allow, cooperate with, and desire the Father to prune back our activities (all the stuff we are doing), so that we can receive plenty of the Son and the Holy Spirit to produce His desired fruit. Without this space, the growth that seems really good to us (and measured as good by the world and even by the church) actually causes us to dry up, wither, and have no fruit. This describes us so well in becoming weary, worn out, even burned out with our good activities. We all need to pay attention to this big invitation by the Father to cut back, cut back, cut back. Do not think it is disappointing to God or being selfish. On the contrary, it is His perfect will for the fruit He plans and desires.

2. FRUIT: This one caught us by surprise. If the fruit (bunches of grapes) on the branches is so much so that it touches each other, they rot, become mushy, and are worthless. This "touching of bunches of grapes" does not allow the air needed for the grapes to continue its proper completion; and through this lack of air, they cause each other to rot. The fruit also needs "space," or it becomes worthless.

Key revelation: We always thought that much fruit meant as much fruit as possible and seems like that would be a good thing. Not so. When the fruit gets too much, it causes all of what's on that branch to rot. Wow, even the fruit needs to be managed and given plenty of space. Thus, we are not in any way to view the magnitude of our fruit as our responsibility or think that more is better. Rather, it is about what the Vinedresser desires and trusting that He knows what is optimal for us. Our fruit is to be discrete, and thus, not all forced together making it seem even bigger. Further, that the fruit is individual so having large groups where there is no space for the fruit to thrive causes the very fruit produced to rot and be worthless. This means to us that we will not actually know the fruit that God brings through our being faithful and just abiding, but by allowing Him to prune and bring His desired fruit. We believe this speaks to multiplication and that our real ministry fruit is helping those who God brings across our path to experience us receiving the amazing fruit of transformation and supernatural work. They themselves then want to get connected to the Vine and learn to abide, as well as to learn the lessons of pruning through space and margin. It is a big reorientation of our role, our willingness to let the Father prune us for this space and margin and understand that the very fruit of those who become fruit is produced for them to get connected with others and enjoy the life of abiding. This is very profound, but not easy to grasp.

What do these verses state about pruning? What happens when branches are pruned? Why?

---

**Read John 15:1–5:**

I Am the True Vine

**15** "I am the true vine, and my Father is the vinedresser. [2] Every branch in me that does not bear fruit he takes away, and every branch that does bear fruit he prunes, that it may bear more fruit. [3] Already you are clean because of the word that I have spoken to you. [4] Abide in me, and I in you. As the branch cannot bear fruit by itself, unless it abides in the vine, neither can you, unless you abide in me. [5] I am the vine; you are the branches. Whoever abides in me and I in him, he it is that bears much fruit, for apart from me you can do nothing.

---

_______________________________________________

_______________________________________________

_______________________________________________

_______________________________________________

_______________________________________________

Who is responsible for pruning? How does He do this?

---

**Read Hebrews 13:20–21:**

Benediction

[20] Now may the God of peace who brought again from the dead our Lord Jesus, the great shepherd of the sheep, by the blood of the eternal covenant, [21] equip you with everything good that you may do his will, working in us[a] that which is pleasing in his sight, through Jesus Christ, to whom be glory forever and ever. Amen.

---

_______________________________________________

_______________________________________________

_______________________________________________

_______________________________________________

_______________________________________________

What does He say about not being entangled in civilian affairs? What does this mean practically to us as believers and followers of Christ?

---

**Read 2 Timothy 2:1–7:**

A Good Soldier of Christ Jesus

**2** then, my child, be strengthened by the grace that is in Christ Jesus, [2] and what you have heard from me in the presence of many witnesses entrust to faithful men,[a] who will be able to teach others also. [3] Share in suffering as a good soldier of Christ Jesus. [4] No soldier gets entangled in civilian pursuits, since his aim is to please the one who enlisted him. [5] An athlete is not crowned unless he competes

---

> according to the rules. [6] It is the hard-working farmer who ought to have the first share of the crops. [7] Think over what I say, for the Lord will give you understanding in everything.

---

## SELF-CENTEREDNESS

What are the consequences of our self-centeredness? Why is this significant to our lives? Why are we self-centered?

**Read James 1:12–18:**

[12] Blessed is the man who remains steadfast under trial, for when he has stood the test he will receive the crown of life, which God has promised to those who love him. [13] Let no one say when he is tempted, "I am being tempted by God," for God cannot be tempted with evil, and he himself tempts no one. [14] But each person is tempted when he is lured and enticed by his own desire. [15] Then desire when it has conceived gives birth to sin, and sin when it is fully grown brings forth death.

[16] Do not be deceived, my beloved brothers. [17] Every good gift and every perfect gift is from above, coming down from the Father of lights, with whom there is no variation or shadow due to change.[a] [18] Of his own will he brought us forth by the word of truth, that we should be a kind of firstfruits of his creatures.

What causes our conflicts and quarrels? Underneath this is a more profound reason for difficulties. What are they? Why do we as believers experience these?

---

**Read James 4:1–5:**

Warning Against Worldliness

**4** What causes quarrels and what causes fights among you? Is it not this, that your passions[a] are at war within you?[b] 2 You desire and do not have, so you murder. You covet and cannot obtain, so you fight and quarrel. You do not have, because you do not ask. 3 You ask and do not receive, because you ask wrongly, to spend it on your passions. 4 You adulterous people![c] Do you not know that friendship with the world is enmity with God? Therefore whoever wishes to be a friend of the world makes himself an enemy of God. 5 Or do you suppose it is to no purpose that the Scripture says, "He yearns jealously over the spirit that he has made to dwell in us"?

---

______________________________________________________

______________________________________________________

______________________________________________________

______________________________________________________

______________________________________________________

What are the reasons we are considered foolish? What are the consequences?

---

**Read Proverbs 18:1–2:**

**18** Whoever isolates himself seeks his own desire;
    he breaks out against all sound judgment.
2 A fool takes no pleasure in understanding,
    but only in expressing his opinion.

---

_______________________________________________

_______________________________________________

_______________________________________________

_______________________________________________

_______________________________________________

What problem does haste cause? Why do we tend to go too fast?

**Read Proverbs 19:2–3:**

2 Desire[a] without knowledge is not good,
   and whoever makes haste with his feet misses his way.
3 When a man's folly brings his way to ruin,
   his heart rages against the Lord.

_______________________________________________

_______________________________________________

_______________________________________________

_______________________________________________

_______________________________________________

As a believer, we do attempt to spend time in the Word, but often it has no affect and contributes to our adversity. Why is this and what does this look like in our lives?

**Read Mark 4:13–19:**

13 And he said to them, "Do you not understand this parable? How then will you understand all the parables? 14 The sower sows the word. 15 And these are the ones along the path, where the word is sown: when they hear, Satan immediately comes and takes away the word that is sown in them. 16 And these are the ones sown on rocky ground: the ones who, when they hear the word, immediately receive it with joy. 17 And they have no root in themselves, but endure for a while; then, when tribulation or persecution arises on account of the word, immediately they fall away.[a] 18 And others are the ones sown among

> thorns. They are those who hear the word, [19] but the cares of the world and the deceitfulness of riches and the desires for other things enter in and choke the word, and it proves unfruitful.

______________________________________________

______________________________________________

______________________________________________

______________________________________________

______________________________________________

In these verses, what are the scenarios that cause adversity? What do these look like in our lives?

**Read Psalm 107:4–5; 10–12; 17–18:**

[4] Some wandered in desert wastes,
    finding no way to a city to dwell in;
[5] hungry and thirsty,
    their soul fainted within them.

[10] Some sat in darkness and in the shadow of death,
    prisoners in affliction and in irons,
[11] for they had rebelled against the words of God,
    and spurned the counsel of the Most High.
[12] So he bowed their hearts down with hard labor;
    they fell down, with none to help.
[17] Some were fools through their sinful ways,
    and because of their iniquities suffered affliction;
[18] they loathed any kind of food,
    and they drew near to the gates of death.

______________________________________________

______________________________________________

______________________________________________

______________________________________________

______________________________________________

What does being in the carnal mean? What are the consequences of being in the carnal? Why is this so significant to our problems of adversity?

> **Read Romans 8:5–8:**
>
> 5 For those who live according to the flesh set their minds on the things of the flesh, but those who live according to the Spirit set their minds on the things of the Spirit. 6 For to set the mind on the flesh is death, but to set the mind on the Spirit is life and peace. 7 For the mind that is set on the flesh is hostile to God, for it does not submit to God's law; indeed, it cannot. 8 Those who are in the flesh cannot please God.

______________________________________________

______________________________________________

______________________________________________

______________________________________________

______________________________________________

What does being selfish cause? How is chasing riches selfish? What does that mean when we are to work and earn money and need money to function in life?

> **Read 1 Timothy 6:9–10:**
>
> 9 But those who desire to be rich fall into temptation, into a snare, into many senseless and harmful desires that plunge people into ruin and destruction. 10 For the love of money is a root of all kinds of evils. It is through this craving that some have wandered away from the faith and pierced themselves with many pangs.

______________________________________________

______________________________________________

______________________________________________

______________________________________________

______________________________________________

What causes separation from God? Why? What does this look like for us personally?

---

**Read Isaiah 59:1–2:**

Evil and Oppression

59 Behold, the Lord's hand is not shortened, that it cannot save,
or his ear dull, that it cannot hear;
2 but your iniquities have made a separation
between you and your God,
and your sins have hidden his face from you
so that he does not hear.

---

_______________________________________________

_______________________________________________

_______________________________________________

_______________________________________________

_______________________________________________

> **" The Scriptures tell us not to be discouraged in situations where discipline is necessary."**

## DISCIPLINE

What do these verses tell us about God's purpose in discipline? What causes discipline? How does this apply to us?

> **Read Hebrews 12:5–7:**
>
> [5] And have you forgotten the exhortation that addresses you as sons?
> "My son, do not regard lightly the discipline of the Lord,
>      nor be weary when reproved by him.
> [6] For the Lord disciplines the one he loves,
>      and chastises every son whom he receives."
> [7] It is for discipline that you have to endure. God is treating you as sons. For what son is there whom his father does not discipline?

What is correction about? Why? Why is it necessary? How does it apply to us?

> **Read Proverbs 3:11–12:**
>
> [11] My son, do not despise the Lord's discipline
>    or be weary of his reproof,
> [12] for the Lord reproves him whom he loves,
>    as a father the son in whom he delights.

_______________________________________________

_______________________________________________

_______________________________________________

_______________________________________________

_______________________________________________

What was the problem with the church? Why did it require discipline? What was offered? What does this mean to us?

> **Read Revelation 3:14–22:**
>
> To the Church in Laodicea
> [14] "And to the angel of the church in Laodicea write: 'The words of the Amen, the faithful and true witness, the beginning of God's creation.
> [15] "'I know your works: you are neither cold nor hot. Would that you were either cold or hot! [16] So, because you are lukewarm, and neither hot nor cold, I will spit you out of my mouth. [17] For you say, I am rich, I have prospered, and I need nothing, not realizing that you are wretched, pitiable, poor, blind, and naked. [18] I counsel you to buy from me gold refined by fire, so that you may be rich, and white garments so that you may clothe yourself and the shame of your nakedness may not be seen, and salve to anoint your eyes, so that you may see. [19] Those whom I love, I reprove and discipline, so be zealous and repent. [20] Behold, I stand at the door and knock. If anyone hears my voice and opens the door, I will come in to him and eat with him, and he with me. [21] The one who conquers, I will grant him to sit with me on my throne, as I also conquered and sat down with my Father on his throne. [22] He who has an ear, let him hear what the Spirit says to the churches.'"

_______________________________________________

_______________________________________________

_______________________________________________

_______________________________________________

_______________________________________________

Why did the psalmist appreciate being disciplined? What does it say about God's reasons for discipline?  How does this apply to us?

**Read Psalm 119:65–72:**

Teth

[65] You have dealt well with your servant,
   O Lord, according to your word.
[66] Teach me good judgment and knowledge,
   for I believe in your commandments.
[67] Before I was afflicted I went astray,
   but now I keep your word.
[68] You are good and do good;
   teach me your statutes.
[69] The insolent smear me with lies,
   but with my whole heart I keep your precepts;
[70] their heart is unfeeling like fat,
   but I delight in your law.
[71] It is good for me that I was afflicted,
   that I might learn your statutes.
[72] The law of your mouth is better to me
   than thousands of gold and silver pieces.

_______________________________________________

_______________________________________________

_______________________________________________

_______________________________________________

_______________________________________________

### JUDGEMENT

What are the reasons for judgment? What exactly is judgment? How does this apply to us?

---

**Read Jeremiah 1:15–16:**

[15] For behold, I am calling all the tribes of the kingdoms of the north, declares the Lord, and they shall come, and every one shall set his throne at the entrance of the gates of Jerusalem, against all its walls all around and against all the cities of Judah. [16] And I will declare my judgments against them, for all their evil in forsaking me. They have made offerings to other gods and worshiped the works of their own hands.

---

____________________________________________________________

____________________________________________________________

____________________________________________________________

____________________________________________________________

____________________________________________________________

What are further reasons for judgment? What are these practically in our lives?

---

**Read Jeremiah 7:24–34:**

[24] But they did not obey or incline their ear, but walked in their own counsels and the stubbornness of their evil hearts, and went backward and not forward. [25] From the day that your fathers came out of the land of Egypt to this day, I have persistently sent all my servants the prophets to them, day after day. [26] Yet they did not listen to me or incline their ear, but stiffened their neck. They did worse than their fathers.

[27] "So you shall speak all these words to them, but they will not listen to you. You shall call to them, but they will not answer you. [28] And you shall say to them, 'This is the nation that did not obey the voice of the Lord their God, and did not accept discipline; truth has perished; it is cut off from their lips.

29 "'Cut off your hair and cast it away;
    raise a lamentation on the bare heights,
for the Lord has rejected and forsaken
    the generation of his wrath.'

**The Valley of Slaughter**

30 "For the sons of Judah have done evil in my sight, declares the Lord. They have set their detestable things in the house that is called by my name, to defile it. 31 And they have built the high places of Topheth, which is in the Valley of the Son of Hinnom, to burn their sons and their daughters in the fire, which I did not command, nor did it come into my mind. 32 Therefore, behold, the days are coming, declares the Lord, when it will no more be called Topheth, or the Valley of the Son of Hinnom, but the Valley of Slaughter; for they will bury in Topheth, because there is no room elsewhere. 33 And the dead bodies of this people will be food for the birds of the air, and for the beasts of the earth, and none will frighten them away. 34 And I will silence in the cities of Judah and in the streets of Jerusalem the voice of mirth and the voice of gladness, the voice of the bridegroom and the voice of the bride, for the land shall become a waste.

___________________________________________
___________________________________________
___________________________________________
___________________________________________
___________________________________________

How do these "Christmas" verses describe Christ's government? What role does judgment have? Why is this important for us to live out?

**Read Isaiah 9:6–7:**

6 For to us a child is born,
    to us a son is given;
and the government shall be upon[a] his shoulder,
    and his name shall be called[b]
Wonderful Counselor, Mighty God,
    Everlasting Father, Prince of Peace.

> [7] Of the increase of his government and of peace
>    there will be no end,
> on the throne of David and over his kingdom,
>    to establish it and to uphold it
> with justice and with righteousness
>    from this time forth and forevermore.
> The zeal of the Lord of hosts will do this.

---

## ATTACK OF SATAN

How does this verse describe Satan? What does that mean in our lives?

> **Read 1 Peter 5:8:**
>
> [8] Be sober-minded; be watchful. Your adversary the devil prowls around like a roaring lion, seeking someone to devour.

---

What are we fighting against? Why is this important to understand in our lives? What schemes do they use, and how do we experience these?

> **Read Ephesians 6:10–12:**
>
> The Whole Armor of God
> [10] Finally, be strong in the Lord and in the strength of his might. [11] Put on the whole armor of God, that you may be able to stand against the schemes of the devil. [12] For we do not wrestle against flesh and blood, but against the rulers, against the authorities, against the cosmic powers over this present darkness, against the spiritual forces of evil in the heavenly places.

________________________________________

________________________________________

________________________________________

________________________________________

________________________________________

What is always with us? Why is this important to understand? How are we to approach this problem?

> **Read Matthew 13:36–43:**
>
> The Parable of the Weeds Explained
> [36] Then he left the crowds and went into the house. And his disciples came to him, saying, "Explain to us the parable of the weeds of the field." [37] He answered, "The one who sows the good seed is the Son of Man. [38] The field is the world, and the good seed is the sons of the kingdom. The weeds are the sons of the evil one, [39] and the enemy who sowed them is the devil. The harvest is the end of the age, and the reapers are angels. [40] Just as the weeds are gathered and burned with fire, so will it be at the end of the age. [41] The Son of Man will send his angels, and they will gather out of his kingdom all causes of sin and all law-breakers, [42] and throw them into the fiery furnace. In that place there will be weeping and gnashing of teeth. [43] Then the righteous will shine like the sun in the kingdom of their Father. He who has ears, let him hear.

_______________________________________________

_______________________________________________

_______________________________________________

_______________________________________________

_______________________________________________

How could Christ call Peter, who just previously was recognized the "rock of the church," now equivalent to Satan? What is important to understand about this in our own lives?

---

**Read Matthew 16:21–23:**

Jesus Foretells His Death and Resurrection

[21] From that time Jesus began to show his disciples that he must go to Jerusalem and suffer many things from the elders and chief priests and scribes, and be killed, and on the third day be raised. [22] And Peter took him aside and began to rebuke him, saying, "Far be it from you, Lord![a] This shall never happen to you." [23] But he turned and said to Peter, "Get behind me, Satan! You are a hindrance[b] to me. For you are not setting your mind on the things of God, but on the things of man."

---

_______________________________________________

_______________________________________________

_______________________________________________

_______________________________________________

_______________________________________________

# LESSON 4:
## CAUSES OF ADVERSITY (CONTINUED)

### SATAN USES THOSE WHO OPPOSE US.

How does Satan and the demonic use others to draw us away from God and into problems of the world? What exactly happens in these dynamics in our heart? Why?

**Read Ephesians 4:25–31:**

25 Therefore, having put away falsehood, let each one of you speak the truth with his neighbor, for we are members one of another. 26 Be angry and do not sin; do not let the sun go down on your anger, 27 and give no opportunity to the devil.28 Let the thief no longer steal, but rather let him labor, doing honest work with his own hands, so that he may have something to share with anyone in need.29 Let no corrupting talk come out of your mouths, but only such as is good for building up, as fits the occasion, that it may give grace to those who hear. 30 And do not grieve the Holy Spirit of God, by whom you were sealed for the day of redemption. 31 Let all bitterness and wrath and anger and clamor and slander be put away from you, along with all malice.

_______________________________________________

_______________________________________________

_______________________________________________

_______________________________________________

_______________________________________________

What specifically do people do to attack us? How does this work and why does this work? What causes us problems and why?

**Read Psalm 7:1–2, 14:**

In You Do I Take Refuge
A Shiggaion[a] of David, which he sang to the Lord concerning the words of Cush, a Benjaminite.
7 O Lord my God, in you do I take refuge;
   save me from all my pursuers and deliver me,
2 lest like a lion they tear my soul apart,

> rending it in pieces, with none to deliver.
> [14] Behold, the wicked man conceives evil
> and is pregnant with mischief
> and gives birth to lies.

______________________________________________

______________________________________________

______________________________________________

______________________________________________

______________________________________________

In this story of Goliath, how does an enemy come against us, and what is a typical response? Why is this a problem? What is the enemy attempting to do? Why?

**Read 1 Samuel 17:1–26:**

David and Goliath

**17** Now the Philistines gathered their armies for battle. And they were gathered at Socoh, which belongs to Judah, and encamped between Socoh and Azekah, in Ephes-dammim. [2] And Saul and the men of Israel were gathered, and encamped in the Valley of Elah, and drew up in line of battle against the Philistines. [3] And the Philistines stood on the mountain on the one side, and Israel stood on the mountain on the other side, with a valley between them. [4] And there came out from the camp of the Philistines a champion named Goliath of Gath, whose height was six[a] cubits[b] and a span. [5] He had a helmet of bronze on his head, and he was armed with a coat of mail, and the weight of the coat was five thousand shekels[c] of bronze. [6] And he had bronze armor on his legs, and a javelin of bronze slung between his shoulders. [7] The shaft of his spear was like a weaver's beam, and his spear's head weighed six hundred shekels of iron. And his shield-bearer went before him. [8] He stood and shouted to the ranks of Israel, "Why have you come out to draw up for battle? Am I not a Philistine, and are you not servants of Saul? Choose a man for yourselves, and let him come down to me. [9] If he is able to fight with me and kill me, then we will be your servants. But if I prevail against him and kill him, then you shall be our servants and serve us." [10] And the Philistine said, "I defy the ranks of Israel this day. Give me a man, that we may fight together." [11] When Saul and all Israel heard these words of the Philistine, they were dismayed and greatly afraid.

<sup>12</sup> Now David was the son of an Ephrathite of Bethlehem in Judah, named Jesse, who had eight sons. In the days of Saul the man was already old and advanced in years.[d] <sup>13</sup> The three oldest sons of Jesse had followed Saul to the battle. And the names of his three sons who went to the battle were Eliab the firstborn, and next to him Abinadab, and the third Shammah. <sup>14</sup> David was the youngest. The three eldest followed Saul, 15 but David went back and forth from Saul to feed his father's sheep at Bethlehem. <sup>16</sup> For forty days the Philistine came forward and took his stand, morning and evening.

<sup>17</sup> And Jesse said to David his son, "Take for your brothers an ephah[e] of this parched grain, and these ten loaves, and carry them quickly to the camp to your brothers. <sup>18</sup> Also take these ten cheeses to the commander of their thousand. See if your brothers are well, and bring some token from them."

<sup>19</sup> Now Saul and they and all the men of Israel were in the Valley of Elah, fighting with the Philistines. <sup>20</sup> And David rose early in the morning and left the sheep with a keeper and took the provisions and went, as Jesse had commanded him. And he came to the encampment as the host was going out to the battle line, shouting the war cry. <sup>21</sup> And Israel and the Philistines drew up for battle, army against army. <sup>22</sup> And David left the things in charge of the keeper of the baggage and ran to the ranks and went and greeted his brothers. <sup>23</sup> As he talked with them, behold, the champion, the Philistine of Gath, Goliath by name, came up out of the ranks of the Philistines and spoke the same words as before. And David heard him.

<sup>24</sup> All the men of Israel, when they saw the man, fled from him and were much afraid. <sup>25</sup> And the men of Israel said, "Have you seen this man who has come up? Surely he has come up to defy Israel. And the king will enrich the man who kills him with great riches and will give him his daughter and make his father's house free in Israel." <sup>26</sup> And David said to the men who stood by him, "What shall be done for the man who kills this Philistine and takes away the reproach from Israel? For who is this uncircumcised Philistine, that he should defy the armies of the living God?"

# LESSON 4:
## CAUSES OF ADVERSITY (CONTINUED)

> **"If we have been invited to repent but have not, then the adversity is becoming more pronounced."**

Usually, we know right away what adversity we are facing especially when we are walking in the Spirit. If we don't know, we are not to second guess, but just proceed according to the wisdom we are receiving as to how the Lord wants to deal with this adversity. Pray through it and respond to God's instructions.

### ABIDING, WALKING IN THE SPIRIT:

1. **Is this general adversity?** Is this a simple frustration that is not against me personally, but comes because I live in a world controlled by Satan, a world of steal, kill, and destroy, a world of entropy that is falling apart and filled with self-centered people? It should not surprise me, and normally my days will experience frustration and things that do not work perfectly as the things I own and have will break down.

2. **Is this a test of faith?** We will know if we have been receiving Rhema Words from God—promises, prophetic foretelling or forth-telling, truths of transformation, deliverance, etc. As we are abiding in Him, we know what we are being tested on, and thus, are to cooperate with the test and let Him complete our faith and overcome this adversity through this test of faith.

3. **Is this pruning?** Are we tired, weary, not enjoying our work, our marriage, our family, or our ministry? Then something is wrong, and this adversity is meant to get our attention to allow God to cut back our activities, so we can regain margin and sweetness in our life. We are to fully cooperate.

4. **Is this coming from selfishness?** If we are not abiding in the Vine, in His Word, hearing His voice, or have gone to the flesh through self-determination of selfish, sinful thoughts, then by definition we are walking in the flesh (carnal). Romans 8:5–8 says that when we live in the flesh, we put to death the life of the Spirit in us (as if no effect), are at enmity against God (working against the will of God), and cannot please God (not enjoying God's life and purposes in and for us). In essence then, our adversities will be coming from selfishness. We have left the Kingdom of God because we are exercising our will and not surrendering to the King and His will, and

thus have lost our peace, joy, freedom, and perhaps gone to unforgiveness—all indicators that we are not walking in the Spirit, in the Kingdom. We are to repent immediately and return to the relationship of the Spirit and the power of the Kingdom, where God can take authority against this adversity.

5. If we have been invited to repent but have not, then the adversity is becoming more pronounced. **Is it then coming from being disciplined?** The Father wants us to experience the severity of the adversity, so our response will be to repent and decide to return to the relationship of the Spirit and the power of the Kingdom, where God can take authority against this adversity.

6. The adversity has gotten worse, and if we have been invited to repent once again, but have not, then **is this coming from being led into judgment?** The adversity is now leading to even more severe consequences of my life, so we repent and decide to return to the relationship of the Spirit and the power of the Kingdom, where God can take authority against this adversity.

7. **Is this coming from a direct attack from Satan who is coming against me to thwart God's will in my life and cause me to cease following God, thereby taking things back into his own hands?** If so, we are to stand against it so God can take authority against this adversity.

## HOW TO OVERCOME ADVERSITY:

**THE FIRST PRINCIPLE IS WALKING WITH GOD IN ALL THINGS.**
What does Christ say is key to following Him as we seek solutions to adversity? Why is this so critical to the process? Why might it be so difficult?

---

**Read Matthew 10:34–39; 16:24–27:**

Not Peace, but a Sword
34 "Do not think that I have come to bring peace to the earth. I have not come to bring peace, but a sword. 35 For I have come to set a man against his father, and a daughter against her mother, and a daughter-in-law against her mother-in-law. 36 And a person's enemies will be those of his own household. 37 Whoever loves father or mother more than me is not worthy of me, and whoever loves son or daughter more than me is not worthy of me. 38 And whoever does not take his cross and follow me is not worthy of me. 39 Whoever finds his life will lose it, and whoever loses his life for my sake will find it.

---

Take Up Your Cross and Follow Jesus

24 Then Jesus told his disciples, "If anyone would come after me, let him deny himself and take up his cross and follow me. 25 For whoever would save his life[a]will lose it, but whoever loses his life for my sake will find it. 26 For what will it profit a man if he gains the whole world and forfeits his soul? Or what shall a man give in return for his soul? 27 For the Son of Man is going to come with his angels in the glory of his Father, and then he will repay each person according to what he has done.

___________________________________________

___________________________________________

___________________________________________

___________________________________________

___________________________________________

As we seek Him individually, what next is important in the process? Why is this so critical to seeking His answers? What is the benefit to us?

**Read Luke 11:14–23:**

Jesus and Beelzebul

14 Now he was casting out a demon that was mute. When the demon had gone out, the mute man spoke, and the people marveled. 15 But some of them said, "He casts out demons by Beelzebul, the prince of demons," 16 while others, to test him, kept seeking from him a sign from heaven. 17 But he, knowing their thoughts, said to them, "Every kingdom divided against itself is laid waste, and a divided household falls. 18 And if Satan also is divided against himself, how will his kingdom stand? For you say that I cast out demons by Beelzebul. 19 And if I cast out demons by Beelzebul, by whom do your sons cast them out? Therefore they will be your judges. 20 But if it is by the finger of God that I cast out demons, then the kingdom of God has come upon you. 21 When a strong man, fully armed, guards his own palace, his goods are safe; 22 but when one stronger than he attacks him and overcomes him, he takes away his armor in which he trusted and divides his spoil. 23 Whoever is not with me is against me, and whoever does not gather with me scatters.

# LESSON 5:
## HOW DO I KNOW WHICH ADVERSITY I AM FACING?
## HOW DO I OVERCOME THESE ADVERSITIES?

_______________________________________________

_______________________________________________

_______________________________________________

_______________________________________________

_______________________________________________

Now, let's look at the specific responses in order to have God resolve these different adversities that we face. Since they are from different sources, the responses are not all the same, but related to the source:

## 1.  GENERAL ADVERSITY:

**Stay in Peace, in the Kingdom:**
To respond, what is important to properly process the solution to general adversity?

> **Read Romans 14:17:**
>
> [17] For the kingdom of God is not a matter of eating and drinking but of righteousness and peace and joy in the Holy Spirit.

_______________________________________________

_______________________________________________

_______________________________________________

_______________________________________________

_______________________________________________

What does Christ promise as we experience trouble? What does this look like for me?

> **Read John 16:33:**
>
> [33] I have said these things to you, that in me you may have peace. In the world you will have tribulation. But take heart; I have overcome the world."

---

---

---

---

Despite the trouble we encounter, what does God promise? What does this mean to us? How do we react to this?

> **Read Romans 8:28:**
>
> [28] And we know that for those who love God all things work together for good,[a] for those who are called according to his purpose.

---

---

---

---

**Seek Wisdom:**

Then, what are we to seek as we need answers to our adversity? What does God promise? What does this mean to us?

> **Read James 1:5–8:**
>
> [5] If any of you lacks wisdom, let him ask God, who gives generously to all without reproach, and it will be given him. [6] But let him ask in faith, with no doubting, for the one who doubts is like a wave of the sea that is driven and tossed by the wind. [7] For that person must not suppose that he will receive anything from the Lord; [8] he is a double-minded man, unstable in all his ways.

_______________________________________________

_______________________________________________

_______________________________________________

_______________________________________________

_______________________________________________

**Listen/Follow:**

As we ask for wisdom, what is our role? What will He speak, and how specific will it be? Why is this important to us?

> **Read Isaiah 30:18–22:**
>
> The Lord Will Be Gracious
> [18] Therefore the Lord waits to be gracious to you,
>   and therefore he exalts himself to show mercy to you.
> For the Lord is a God of justice;
>   blessed are all those who wait for him.
> [19] For a people shall dwell in Zion, in Jerusalem; you shall weep no more. He will surely be gracious to you at the sound of your cry. As soon as he hears it, he answers you. [20] And though the Lord give you the bread of adversity and the water of affliction, yet your Teacher will not hide himself anymore, but your eyes shall see your Teacher. [21] And your ears shall hear a word behind you, saying, "This is the way, walk in it," when you turn to the right or when you turn to the left. [22] Then you will defile your carved idols overlaid with silver and your gold-plated metal images. You will scatter them as unclean things. You will say to them, "Be gone!"

________________________________________

________________________________________

________________________________________

________________________________________

**Passes Quickly/Frustration over:**
What does He say He will give us, and what should we expect? What does this mean to us about this problem?

> **Read John 14:27:**
>
> 27 Peace I leave with you; my peace I give to you. Not as the world gives do I give to you. Let not your hearts be troubled, neither let them be afraid.

________________________________________

________________________________________

________________________________________

________________________________________

________________________________________

**Do not let it steal your peace or joy:**
How do we handle this adversity? What is important to get through this?

> **Read and practice Isaiah 26:3–4:**
>
> 3 You keep him in perfect peace
>    whose mind is stayed on you,
>    because he trusts in you.
> 4 Trust in the Lord forever,
>    for the Lord God is an everlasting rock.

_______________________________________________
_______________________________________________
_______________________________________________
_______________________________________________
_______________________________________________

**2.  TEST OF FAITH:**

**We have the Spirit through the New Covenant:**
What does God promise us as we go through a test of faith? Why is this so
wonderful for those of us who struggle with faith? How does it work practically?

**Read Jeremiah 31:31–34:**

The New Covenant
**31** "Behold, the days are coming, declares the Lord, when I will make a new
covenant with the house of Israel and the house of Judah, **32** not like the
covenant that I made with their fathers on the day when I took them by the hand
to bring them out of the land of Egypt, my covenant that they broke, though I
was their husband, declares the Lord. **33** For this is the covenant that I will make
with the house of Israel after those days, declares the Lord: I will put my law
within them, and I will write it on their hearts. And I will be their God, and they
shall be my people. **34** And no longer shall each one teach his neighbor and each
his brother, saying, 'Know the Lord,' for they shall all know me, from the least of
them to the greatest, declares the Lord. For I will forgive their iniquity, and I will
remember their sin no more."

_______________________________________________
_______________________________________________
_______________________________________________
_______________________________________________

# LESSON 5:
## HOW DO I KNOW WHICH ADVERSITY I AM FACING?
## HOW DO I OVERCOME THESE ADVERSITIES?

**Secret Revelation:**

What does God promise to give us as we seek to understand faith and what He is speaking to us? Why is this so important to us?

**Read Luke 10:21–24:**

Jesus Rejoices in the Father's Will

21 In that same hour he rejoiced in the Holy Spirit and said, "I thank you, Father, Lord of heaven and earth, that you have hidden these things from the wise and understanding and revealed them to little children; yes, Father, for such was your gracious will.[a] 22 All things have been handed over to me by my Father, and no one knows who the Son is except the Father, or who the Father is except the Son and anyone to whom the Son chooses to reveal him."
23 Then turning to the disciples he said privately, "Blessed are the eyes that see what you see! 24 For I tell you that many prophets and kings desired to see what you see, and did not see it, and to hear what you hear, and did not hear it."

_______________________________________________

_______________________________________________

_______________________________________________

_______________________________________________

_______________________________________________

**Believe that what He has spoken – His words (Rhema) will come to pass:**

What is critical for us to believe about what Christ has authored? Why is this so important to our process?

**Read Joshua 21:43–45:**

43 Thus the Lord gave to Israel all the land that he swore to give to their fathers. And they took possession of it, and they settled there. 44 And the Lord gave them rest on every side just as he had sworn to their fathers. Not one of all their enemies had withstood them, for the Lord had given all their enemies into their hands. 45 Not one word of all the good promises that the Lord had made to the house of Israel had failed; all came to pass.

______________________________

______________________________

______________________________

______________________________

______________________________

**Go to the throne room with boldness.**

What is our great privilege in this process? On what basis is this privilege, and what does God tell us about this privilege? Why is it so critical to us personally and to our struggle with faith?

**Read Hebrews 10:19–25, 35–38:**

The Full Assurance of Faith

19 Therefore, brothers,[a] since we have confidence to enter the holy places by the blood of Jesus, 20 by the new and living way that he opened for us through the curtain, that is, through his flesh, 21 and since we have a great priest over the house of God, 22 let us draw near with a true heart in full assurance of faith, with our hearts sprinkled clean from an evil conscience and our bodies washed with pure water. 23 Let us hold fast the confession of our hope without wavering, for he who promised is faithful. 24 And let us consider how to stir up one another to love and good works, 25 not neglecting to meet together, as is the habit of some, but encouraging one another, and all the more as you see the Day drawing near.

35 Therefore do not throw away your confidence, which has a great reward. 36 For you have need of endurance, so that when you have done the will of God you may receive what is promised. 37 For,
"Yet a little while,
    and the coming one will come and will not delay;
38 but my righteous one shall live by faith,
    and if he shrinks back,
my soul has no pleasure in him."

_______________________________________________

_______________________________________________

_______________________________________________

_______________________________________________

_______________________________________________

What does He remind us about His role in faith? Why is this so important to us and how does this practically work for us?

**Read Hebrews 12:1–2:**

Jesus, Founder and Perfecter of Our Faith
**12** Therefore, since we are surrounded by so great a cloud of witnesses, let us also lay aside every weight, and sin which clings so closely, and let us run with endurance the race that is set before us, ² looking to Jesus, the founder and perfecter of our faith, who for the joy that was set before him endured the cross, despising the shame, and is seated at the right hand of the throne of God.

_______________________________________________

_______________________________________________

_______________________________________________

_______________________________________________

_______________________________________________

In this story of David, how did he get to faith, and what truths did he come to? Why is this so important for us and our process of coming to faith?

**Read 2 Samuel 7:27–29:**

²⁷ For you, O Lord of hosts, the God of Israel, have made this revelation to your servant, saying, 'I will build you a house.' Therefore your servant has found courage to pray this prayer to you. ²⁸ And now, O Lord God, you are God, and your words are true, and you have promised this good thing to your servant. ²⁹ Now therefore may it please you to bless the house of your servant, so that it may continue forever before you. For you, O Lord God, have spoken, and with your blessing shall the house of your servant be blessed forever."

_______________________________________________

_______________________________________________

_______________________________________________

_______________________________________________

_______________________________________________

What are the truths that you take from this story about how Jehoshaphat dealt with his adversity and went to faith? What is important to you personally?

**Read 2 Chronicles 20:1–30:**

Jehoshaphat's Prayer

**20** After this the Moabites and Ammonites, and with them some of the Meunites,[a] came against Jehoshaphat for battle. [2] Some men came and told Jehoshaphat, "A great multitude is coming against you from Edom,[b] from beyond the sea; and, behold, they are in Hazazon-tamar" (that is, Engedi).[3] Then Jehoshaphat was afraid and set his face to seek the Lord, and proclaimed a fast throughout all Judah. [4] And Judah assembled to seek help from the Lord; from all the cities of Judah they came to seek the Lord.

[5] And Jehoshaphat stood in the assembly of Judah and Jerusalem, in the house of the Lord, before the new court, [6] and said, "O Lord, God of our fathers, are you not God in heaven? You rule over all the kingdoms of the nations. In your hand are power and might, so that none is able to withstand you. [7] Did you not, our God, drive out the inhabitants of this land before your people Israel, and give it forever to the descendants of Abraham your friend? [8] And they have lived in it and have built for you in it a sanctuary for your name, saying, [9] 'If disaster comes upon us, the sword, judgment,[c] or pestilence, or famine, we will stand before this house and before you—for your name is in this house—and cry out to you in our affliction, and you will hear and save.' [10] And now behold, the men of Ammon and Moab and Mount Seir, whom you would not let Israel invade when they came from the land of Egypt, and whom they avoided and did not destroy— [11] behold, they reward us by coming to drive us out of your possession, which you have given us to inherit. [12] O our God, will you not execute judgment on them? For we are powerless against this great horde that is coming against us. We do not know what to do, but our eyes are on you." [13] Meanwhile all Judah stood before the Lord, with their little ones, their wives,

and their children. [14] And the Spirit of the Lord came[d] upon Jahaziel the son of Zechariah, son of Benaiah, son of Jeiel, son of Mattaniah, a Levite of the sons of Asaph, in the midst of the assembly. [15] And he said, "Listen, all Judah and inhabitants of Jerusalem and King Jehoshaphat: Thus says the Lord to you, 'Do not be afraid and do not be dismayed at this great horde, for the battle is not yours but God's. [16] Tomorrow go down against them. Behold, they will come up by the ascent of Ziz. You will find them at the end of the valley, east of the wilderness of Jeruel. [17] You will not need to fight in this battle. Stand firm, hold your position, and see the salvation of the Lord on your behalf, O Judah and Jerusalem.' Do not be afraid and do not be dismayed. Tomorrow go out against them, and the Lord will be with you."

[18] Then Jehoshaphat bowed his head with his face to the ground, and all Judah and the inhabitants of Jerusalem fell down before the Lord, worshiping the Lord. [19] And the Levites, of the Kohathites and the Korahites, stood up to praise the Lord, the God of Israel, with a very loud voice.

[20] And they rose early in the morning and went out into the wilderness of Tekoa. And when they went out, Jehoshaphat stood and said, "Hear me, Judah and inhabitants of Jerusalem! Believe in the Lord your God, and you will be established; believe his prophets, and you will succeed." [21] And when he had taken counsel with the people, he appointed those who were to sing to the Lord and praise him in holy attire, as they went before the army, and say,
"Give thanks to the Lord,
 for his steadfast love endures forever."
[22] And when they began to sing and praise, the Lord set an ambush against the men of Ammon, Moab, and Mount Seir, who had come against Judah, so that they were routed. [23] For the men of Ammon and Moab rose against the inhabitants of Mount Seir, devoting them to destruction, and when they had made an end of the inhabitants of Seir, they all helped to destroy one another.

The Lord Delivers Judah
[24] When Judah came to the watchtower of the wilderness, they looked toward the horde, and behold, there[e] were dead bodies lying on the ground; none had escaped. [25] When Jehoshaphat and his people came to take their spoil, they found among them, in great numbers, goods, clothing, and precious things, which they took for themselves until they could carry no more. They were three days in taking the spoil, it was so much. [26] On the fourth day they assembled in the Valley of Beracah,[f] for there they blessed the Lord. Therefore

the name of that place has been called the Valley of Beracah to this day. [27] Then they returned, every man of Judah and Jerusalem, and Jehoshaphat at their head, returning to Jerusalem with joy, for the Lord had made them rejoice over their enemies. [28] They came to Jerusalem with harps and lyres and trumpets, to the house of the Lord. [29] And the fear of God came on all the kingdoms of the countries when they heard that the Lord had fought against the enemies of Israel. [30] So the realm of Jehoshaphat was quiet, for his God gave him rest all around.

Let's look at our response to God's work in our lives regarding pruning and some of the adversity that we might be experiencing because we are not responding to that pruning.

## PRUNING

Fully cooperate with the Father when He is asking you to open up space and margin, and release burdens to live a life of freedom. What has to be cut back (especially what we may consider to be good things but are not God's things right now) to create fruit, more fruit, much fruit?

Look again at the roles of each of Jesus' spiritual analogies as related to the vineyard, vine, the grapes, and wine making:

**"The vinedresser is the one who has the plan and decides everything about the vineyard including which grapes to grow, how much to water, when to pick, how to process, etc. "**

**Read John 15:1–5:**

I Am the True Vine

**15** "I am the true vine, and my Father is the vinedresser. [2] Every branch in me that does not bear fruit he takes away, and every branch that does bear fruit he prunes, that it may bear more fruit. [3] Already you are clean because of the word that I have spoken to you. [4] Abide in me, and I in you. As the branch cannot bear fruit by itself, unless it abides in the vine, neither can you, unless you abide in me. [5] I am the vine; you are the branches. Whoever abides in me and I in him, he it is that bears much fruit, for apart from me you can do nothing.

**The Vine (Christ):** The vine provides the life – the nutrients, the sap that produces the fruit. (Note that the sap is the Holy Spirit in this analogy).

**The Vinedresser (The Father):** The vinedresser is the one who has the plan and decides everything about the vineyard including which grapes to grow, how much to water, when to pick, how to process, etc. He thus is the one that I term "directing traffic" in all of our lives. He knows and wants to lead us. He is the vinedresser, and we are not.

**The Branch:** A tender and flexible branch. As a branch, we stay connected to the vine to produce fruit, but are not the vine or the vinedresser.

**The Result:** The desire of the vinedresser (the Father) is the fruit – more fruit, much fruit. He does not care about what the vineyard or the branches look like, but only the results: fruit.

> **bear:** to bring, bring to, bring forward
> **fruit:** effect
> **result:** greater in quantity, quality, superior, more excellent

**The Choice:** to remain, abide.

### APART FROM CHRIST WE CAN DO NOTHING!

Repeat this over and over. Apart from abiding, we can do nothing. And it is our choice. We must decide that abiding is something we wish to learn and live out now and for the rest of our days.

**Word Definition:** **abide:** in reference to place—to sojourn, tarry, not to depart, to continue to be present, to be held, kept, continually

He clearly says that as each plays out their role, one of the key activities is for us (the branches) to be pruned. This means we are to cut back our activities that overwhelm us, so that we have margin, space in our lives for the process of fruit bearing to be full, luscious, enjoyable, and all that God wants it to be. Pruning is absolutely required for all healthy branches to be able to bear fruit. None of us is exempt, and we are to fully cooperate with this process. If not, we get tired and weary, and God will bring adversity to cause us to have a heart to cooperate so that we are pruned and able to enjoy our lives to the fullest.

As you consider pruning, what is the key to letting God create the good works since you are His workmanship? How does this practically work?

---

**Read Ephesians 2:10:**

¹⁰ For we are his workmanship, created in Christ Jesus for good works, which God prepared beforehand, that we should walk in them.

---

________________________________________

________________________________________

________________________________________

________________________________________

________________________________________

**Seek Wisdom:**

As we look at this verse again in light of pruning, what specifically are you to seek wisdom about in relation to your activities?

**Read James 1:5–8:**

5 If any of you lacks wisdom, let him ask God, who gives generously to all without reproach, and it will be given him. 6 But let him ask in faith, with no doubting, for the one who doubts is like a wave of the sea that is driven and tossed by the wind. 7 For that person must not suppose that he will receive anything from the Lord; 8 he is a double-minded man, unstable in all his ways.

________________________________________

________________________________________

________________________________________

________________________________________

________________________________________

## SELFISHNESS/DISCIPLINE/JUDGEMENT:

What caused selfishness, and how was it overcome? What does this mean to us regarding how to repent and get into the right relationship to have God resolve our adversity?

**Read Romans 5:12–21:**

Death in Adam, Life in Christ

12 Therefore, just as sin came into the world through one man, and death through sin, and so death spread to all men[a] because all sinned— 13 for sin indeed was in the world before the law was given, but sin is not counted where

there is no law.[14] Yet death reigned from Adam to Moses, even over those whose sinning was not like the transgression of Adam, who was a type of the one who was to come.

[15] But the free gift is not like the trespass. For if many died through one man's trespass, much more have the grace of God and the free gift by the grace of that one man Jesus Christ abounded for many. [16] And the free gift is not like the result of that one man's sin. For the judgment following one trespass brought condemnation, but the free gift following many trespasses brought justification.[17] For if, because of one man's trespass, death reigned through that one man, much more will those who receive the abundance of grace and the free gift of righteousness reign in life through the one man Jesus Christ.

[18] Therefore, as one trespass[b] led to condemnation for all men, so one act of righteousness[c] leads to justification and life for all men. [19] For as by the one man's disobedience the many were made sinners, so by the one man's obedience the many will be made righteous. [20] Now the law came in to increase the trespass, but where sin increased, grace abounded all the more, [21] so that, as sin reigned in death, grace also might reign through righteousness leading to eternal life through Jesus Christ our Lord.

_______________________________________________

_______________________________________________

_______________________________________________

_______________________________________________

_______________________________________________

What is the process of repentance? What does it result in, and why is this so important to our process of Him resolving our adversity?

> **Read 1 John 1:9:**
>
> [9] If we confess our sins, he is faithful and just to forgive us our sins and to cleanse us from all unrighteousness.

_______________________________________________

_______________________________________________

_______________________________________________

_______________________________________________

_______________________________________________

Identify the progression to a life of fruit and resolution to adversity. What is the key to having it fulfilled for us? (It is a paradox.)

> **Read Romans 6:7, 18, 22:**
>
> [7] For one who has died has been set free[a] from sin.
>
> [18] and, having been set free from sin, have become slaves of righteousness.
>
> [22] But now that you have been set free from sin and have become slaves of God, the fruit you get leads to sanctification and its end, eternal life.

_______________________________________________

_______________________________________________

_______________________________________________

_______________________________________________

_______________________________________________

What are God's promises to restoring us from our adversities that we caused? Why is this so important for our process, and what can we expect?

> **Read Ezekiel 36:33–38:**
>
> [33] "Thus says the Lord God: On the day that I cleanse you from all your iniquities, I will cause the cities to be inhabited, and the waste places shall be rebuilt.[34] And the land that was desolate shall be tilled, instead of being the desolation that it was in the sight of all who passed by. [35] And they will say, 'This land that was desolate has become like the garden of Eden, and the waste and desolate and ruined cities are now fortified and inhabited.' [36] Then the nations that are left all around you shall know that I am the Lord; I have rebuilt the ruined places and replanted that which was desolate. I am the Lord; I have spoken, and I will do it.
>
> [37] "Thus says the Lord God: This also I will let the house of Israel ask me to do for them: to increase their people like a flock. [38] Like the flock for sacrifices,[a]like the flock at Jerusalem during her appointed feasts, so shall the waste cities be filled with flocks of people. Then they will know that I am the Lord."

_________________________________________________

_________________________________________________

_________________________________________________

_________________________________________________

# LESSON 6:
## OVERCOMING ADVERSITIES (CONTINUED)

When we are stuck and seemingly have no options for resolution, what does God promise? Why is this so important to our heart and to the process of resolution?

**Read Psalm 40:1–8:**

My Help and My Deliverer
To the choirmaster. A Psalm of David.
**40** I waited patiently for the Lord;
  he inclined to me and heard my cry.
[2] He drew me up from the pit of destruction,
  out of the miry bog,
and set my feet upon a rock,
  making my steps secure.
[3] He put a new song in my mouth,
  a song of praise to our God.
Many will see and fear,
  and put their trust in the Lord.
[4] Blessed is the man who makes
  the Lord his trust,
who does not turn to the proud,
  to those who go astray after a lie!
[5] You have multiplied, O Lord my God,
  your wondrous deeds and your thoughts toward us;
  none can compare with you!
I will proclaim and tell of them,
  yet they are more than can be told.
[6] In sacrifice and offering you have not delighted,
  but you have given me an open ear.[a]
Burnt offering and sin offering
  you have not required.
[7] Then I said, "Behold, I have come;
  in the scroll of the book it is written of me:
[8] I delight to do your will, O my God;
  your law is within my heart."

_________________________________________________

_________________________________________________

_________________________________________________

_________________________________________________

_________________________________________________

As we are seeking resolution to our adversities, what else does God promise, and why is this so important to our process of realizing resolution?

---

**Read Jeremiah 32:36–41; 33:3–14:**

They Shall Be My People; I Will Be Their God

36 "Now therefore thus says the Lord, the God of Israel, concerning this city of which you say, 'It is given into the hand of the king of Babylon by sword, by famine, and by pestilence': 37 Behold, I will gather them from all the countries to which I drove them in my anger and my wrath and in great indignation. I will bring them back to this place, and I will make them dwell in safety. 38 And they shall be my people, and I will be their God. 39 I will give them one heart and one way, that they may fear me forever, for their own good and the good of their children after them. 40 I will make with them an everlasting covenant, that I will not turn away from doing good to them. And I will put the fear of me in their hearts, that they may not turn from me. 41 I will rejoice in doing them good, and I will plant them in this land in faithfulness, with all my heart and all my soul.

3 Call to me and I will answer you, and will tell you great and hidden things that you have not known. 4 For thus says the Lord, the God of Israel, concerning the houses of this city and the houses of the kings of Judah that were torn down to make a defense against the siege mounds and against the sword: 5 They are coming in to fight against the Chaldeans and to fill them[a] with the dead bodies of men whom I shall strike down in my anger and my wrath, for I have hidden my face from this city because of all their evil. 6 Behold, I will bring to it health and healing, and I will heal them and reveal to them abundance of prosperity and security. 7 I will restore the fortunes of Judah and the fortunes of Israel, and rebuild them as they were at first. 8 I will cleanse them from all the guilt of their sin against me, and I will forgive all the guilt of their sin and rebellion against me. 9 And this city[b] shall be to me a name of joy, a praise and a glory before all the nations of the earth who shall hear of all the good that I do for them. They shall fear and tremble because of all the good and all the prosperity I provide for it.

---

> [10] "Thus says the Lord: In this place of which you say, 'It is a waste without man or beast,' in the cities of Judah and the streets of Jerusalem that are desolate, without man or inhabitant or beast, there shall be heard again [11] the voice of mirth and the voice of gladness, the voice of the bridegroom and the voice of the bride, the voices of those who sing, as they bring thank offerings to the house of the Lord:
>
> "'Give thanks to the Lord of hosts,
>     for the Lord is good,
>     for his steadfast love endures forever!'
> For I will restore the fortunes of the land as at first, says the Lord.
> [12] "Thus says the Lord of hosts: In this place that is waste, without man or beast, and in all of its cities, there shall again be habitations of shepherds resting their flocks. [13] In the cities of the hill country, in the cities of the Shephelah, and in the cities of the Negeb, in the land of Benjamin, the places about Jerusalem, and in the cities of Judah, flocks shall again pass under the hands of the one who counts them, says the Lord.
>
> The Lord's Eternal Covenant with David
> [14] "Behold, the days are coming, declares the Lord, when I will fulfill the promise I made to the house of Israel and the house of Judah.

____________________________________________

____________________________________________

____________________________________________

____________________________________________

____________________________________________

## ATTACKS OF THE ENEMY

When we are attacked by the enemy, what are our two responses, and what is the result? What should we expect about this adversity?

> **Read James 4:7:**
>
> [7] Submit yourselves therefore to God. Resist the devil, and he will flee from you.

___________________________________________

___________________________________________

___________________________________________

___________________________________________

___________________________________________

As we are to put on the armor of God and not fight the enemy with our own power, what are these elements, and what do they mean? What will happen if we use these weapons?

**Read Ephesians 6:10–20:**

The Whole Armor of God

[10] Finally, be strong in the Lord and in the strength of his might. [11] Put on the whole armor of God, that you may be able to stand against the schemes of the devil. [12] For we do not wrestle against flesh and blood, but against the rulers, against the authorities, against the cosmic powers over this present darkness, against the spiritual forces of evil in the heavenly places. [13] Therefore take up the whole armor of God, that you may be able to withstand in the evil day, and having done all, to stand firm. [14] Stand therefore, having fastened on the belt of truth, and having put on the breastplate of righteousness, [15] and, as shoes for your feet, having put on the readiness given by the gospel of peace. [16] In all circumstances take up the shield of faith, with which you can extinguish all the flaming darts of the evil one; [17] and take the helmet of salvation, and the sword of the Spirit, which is the word of God, [18] praying at all times in the Spirit, with all prayer and supplication. To that end, keep alert with all perseverance, making supplication for all the saints, [19] and also for me, that words may be given to me in opening my mouth boldly to proclaim the mystery of the gospel, [20] for which I am an ambassador in chains, that I may declare it boldly, as I ought to speak.

___________________________________________

___________________________________________

___________________________________________

___________________________________________

Based upon the adversaries you noted that you are encountering right now and that you described in detail on the first day, and the effect they are having on you at this moment, review each step and categorize where they fit regarding the source of the adversity. Remember, the adversity will fall into one of these areas:

- General Adversity
- Trial of God
- Pruning
- Selfishness, Discipline, Judgment
- Attacks of the Enemy – Stand and come against

# LESSON 7:
## TAKING AUTHORITY AGAINST THE ADVERSITY

So, we have discerned what kind of adversity this is, and we have taken the appropriate initial action and approach:

1. General Adversity – Staying in peace, following the Father's wisdom

2. Trial of God – Going to fully cooperate

3. Pruning – Going to fully cooperate and work at margin, release of burdens

4. Selfishness, Discipline, Judgment – Repented; returned to Kingdom

5. Attacks of the Enemy – Stand and come against

In each situation now, we will have types of adversity, different levels and severity of adversity, and different levels of spiritual forces against us. At this point, we are already fully living in the Kingdom of God or have returned to living in the Kingdom of God where our authority rests. The power to overcome truly resides through our life in the spiritual dimension of the Kingdom as we operate in the kingdom of the world where we are experiencing the adversity.

## TYPES OF ADVERSITY:

### 1. RELATIONSHIP ISSUES:

- First, go to, stay in forgiveness.

Why is it so important to go to forgiveness? How does this free us up?

> **Read Mark 11:20–25:**
>
> The Lesson from the Withered Fig Tree
> [20] As they passed by in the morning, they saw the fig tree withered away to its roots. [21] And Peter remembered and

> " The power to overcome truly resides through our life in the spiritual dimension of the Kingdom as we operate in the kingdom of the world where we are experiencing the adversity."

said to him, "Rabbi, look! The fig tree that you cursed has withered." [22] And Jesus answered them, "Have faith in God. [23] Truly, I say to you, whoever says to this mountain, 'Be taken up and thrown into the sea,' and does not doubt in his heart, but believes that what he says will come to pass, it will be done for him. [24] Therefore I tell you, whatever you ask in prayer, believe that you have received[a] it, and it will be yours. [25] And whenever you stand praying, forgive, if you have anything against anyone, so that your Father also who is in heaven may forgive you your trespasses."[b]

_______________________________________________

_______________________________________________

_______________________________________________

_______________________________________________

_______________________________________________

On what basis do we go to forgiveness? Why again is this so important?

**Read Ephesians 4:25–32:**

[25] Therefore, having put away falsehood, let each one of you speak the truth with his neighbor, for we are members one of another. [26] Be angry and do not sin; do not let the sun go down on your anger, [27] and give no opportunity to the devil. [28] Let the thief no longer steal, but rather let him labor, doing honest work with his own hands, so that he may have something to share with anyone in need. [29] Let no corrupting talk come out of your mouths, but only such as is good for building up, as fits the occasion, that it may give grace to those who hear. [30] And do not grieve the Holy Spirit of God, by whom you were sealed for the day of redemption. [31] Let all bitterness and wrath and anger and clamor and slander be put away from you, along with all malice. [32] Be kind to one another, tenderhearted, forgiving one another, as God in Christ forgave you.

_______________________________________________

_______________________________________________

_______________________________________________

_______________________________________________

_______________________________________________

# LESSON 7:
## TAKING AUTHORITY AGAINST THE ADVERSITY

What do I understand about the Covenant regarding relationships, especially those who oppose me? Why is this important?

> **Read Genesis 12:1–3:**
>
> The Call of Abram
>
> **12** Now the Lord said[a] to Abram, "Go from your country[b] and your kindred and your father's house to the land that I will show you. 2 And I will make of you a great nation, and I will bless you and make your name great, so that you will be a blessing. 3 I will bless those who bless you, and him who dishonors you I will curse, and in you all the families of the earth shall be blessed."[c]

_______________________________________________

_______________________________________________

_______________________________________________

_______________________________________________

_______________________________________________

For people who continue to oppose us, continue to harm us, how do we handle them, so we are not trapped by their unhealthiness? What does this look like practically, and how does it really work?

> **Read Romans 12:9–20 and Proverbs 20:22:**
>
> Marks of the True Christian
>
> 9 Let love be genuine. Abhor what is evil; hold fast to what is good. 10 Love one another with brotherly affection. Outdo one another in showing honor. 11 Do not be slothful in zeal, be fervent in spirit,[a] serve the Lord. 12 Rejoice in hope, be patient in tribulation, be constant in prayer. 13 Contribute to the needs of the saints and seek to show hospitality.
>
> 14 Bless those who persecute you; bless and do not curse them. 15 Rejoice with those who rejoice, weep with those who weep. 16 Live in harmony with one another. Do not be haughty, but associate with the lowly.[b] Never be wise in your own sight. 17 Repay no one evil for evil, but give thought to do what is honorable in the sight of all. 18 If possible, so far as it depends on you, live peaceably with all. 19 Beloved, never avenge yourselves, but leave it[c] to the wrath of God, for it is

written, "Vengeance is mine, I will repay, says the Lord." [20] To the contrary, "if your enemy is hungry, feed him; if he is thirsty, give him something to drink; for by so doing you will heap burning coals on his head."

[22] Do not say, "I will repay evil";
    wait for the Lord, and he will deliver you.

_______________________________________________

_______________________________________________

_______________________________________________

_______________________________________________

_______________________________________________

How do we pray regarding those who continually are working to harm us, come against us? What does God promise about this? Can we expect this? Why is this important?

**Read Psalm 54:1–7:**

The Lord Upholds My Life
To the choirmaster: with stringed instruments. A Maskil[a] of David, when the Ziphites went and told Saul, "Is not David hiding among us?"
**54** O God, save me by your name,
    and vindicate me by your might.
[2] O God, hear my prayer;
    give ear to the words of my mouth.
[3] For strangers[b] have risen against me;
    ruthless men seek my life;
    they do not set God before themselves. Selah
[4] Behold, God is my helper;
    the Lord is the upholder of my life.
[5] He will return the evil to my enemies;
    in your faithfulness put an end to them.
[6] With a freewill offering I will sacrifice to you;
    I will give thanks to your name, O Lord, for it is good.
[7] For he has delivered me from every trouble,
    and my eye has looked in triumph on my enemies.

_______________________________________________
_______________________________________________
_______________________________________________
_______________________________________________
_______________________________________________

Further, what can we expect God to do for us regarding the adversity that is being caused by people against us? Why is this important for us and our resolution of adversity?

**Read Psalm 40:11–17:**

11 As for you, O Lord, you will not restrain
    your mercy from me;
your steadfast love and your faithfulness will
    ever preserve me!
12 For evils have encompassed me
    beyond number;
my iniquities have overtaken me,
    and I cannot see;
they are more than the hairs of my head;
    my heart fails me.
13 Be pleased, O Lord, to deliver me!
    O Lord, make haste to help me!
14 Let those be put to shame and disappointed altogether
    who seek to snatch away my life;
let those be turned back and brought to dishonor
    who delight in my hurt!
15 Let those be appalled because of their shame
    who say to me, "Aha, Aha!"
16 But may all who seek you
    rejoice and be glad in you;
may those who love your salvation
    say continually, "Great is the Lord!"
17 As for me, I am poor and needy,
    but the Lord takes thought for me.
You are my help and my deliverer;
    do not delay, O my God!

_______________________________________________

_______________________________________________

_______________________________________________

_______________________________________________

_______________________________________________

How are we to view those who are close to us but coming against us? What does God promise us about this? Why is this important to us?

---

**Read Psalm 41:7–13:**

7 All who hate me whisper together about me;
   they imagine the worst for me.[a]
8 They say, "A deadly thing is poured out[b] on him;
   he will not rise again from where he lies."
9 Even my close friend in whom I trusted,
   who ate my bread, has lifted his heel against me.
10 But you, O Lord, be gracious to me,
   and raise me up, that I may repay them!
11 By this I know that you delight in me:
   my enemy will not shout in triumph over me.
12 But you have upheld me because of my integrity,
   and set me in your presence forever.
13 Blessed be the Lord, the God of Israel,
   from everlasting to everlasting!
Amen and Amen.

---

_______________________________________________

_______________________________________________

_______________________________________________

_______________________________________________

_______________________________________________

## 2. LIFE DIFFICULTIES / HEALTH ISSUES / SURPRISES:

**GET SETTLED ON THIS: GOD'S COVENANT LIFE AND HIS WORD ARE ABSOLUTELY TRUE.**

What does God say about His view of the Covenant? Why is this so important to us and our belief about resolution of the adversity?

**Read Psalm 111:1–10:**

Great Are the Lord's Works
**111** [a] Praise the Lord!
I will give thanks to the Lord with my whole heart,
 in the company of the upright, in the congregation.
2 Great are the works of the Lord,
 studied by all who delight in them.
3 Full of splendor and majesty is his work,
 and his righteousness endures forever.
4 He has caused his wondrous works to be remembered;
 the Lord is gracious and merciful.
5 He provides food for those who fear him;
 he remembers his covenant forever.
6 He has shown his people the power of his works,
 in giving them the inheritance of the nations.
7 The works of his hands are faithful and just;
 all his precepts are trustworthy;
8 they are established forever and ever,
 to be performed with faithfulness and uprightness.
9 He sent redemption to his people;
 he has commanded his covenant forever.
 Holy and awesome is his name!
10 The fear of the Lord is the beginning of wisdom;
 all those who practice it have a good understanding.
 His praise endures forever!

________________________________________

________________________________________

________________________________________

________________________________________

________________________________________

His Covenant is based upon Him speaking His Word. What then is important for us to receive? Why?  How do we do this?

---

**Read Proverbs 16:20–22:**

[20] Whoever gives thought to the word[a] will discover good,
  and blessed is he who trusts in the Lord.
[21] The wise of heart is called discerning,
  and sweetness of speech increases persuasiveness.
[22] Good sense is a fountain of life to him who has it,
  but the instruction of fools is folly.

---

________________________________________

________________________________________

________________________________________

________________________________________

________________________________________

As we are needing encouragement, what does God promise to give us? Why is this so important for us at this time of experiencing adversity?

---

**Read Romans 15:13:**

[13] May the God of hope fill you with all joy and peace in believing, so that by the power of the Holy Spirit you may abound in hope.

---

____________________________________

____________________________________

____________________________________

____________________________________

____________________________________

What does Christ remind us about authority and the importance of authority? How are we to live this out? Why?

**Read Matthew 28:18–20:**

[18] And Jesus came and said to them, "All authority in heaven and on earth has been given to me. [19] Go therefore and make disciples of all nations, baptizing them in[a] the name of the Father and of the Son and of the Holy Spirit,[20] teaching them to observe all that I have commanded you. And behold, I am with you always, to the end of the age."

____________________________________

____________________________________

____________________________________

____________________________________

____________________________________

How does He send us out? What role does authority play in this process? How do we experience the supernatural and why?

**Read Luke 9:1–2; 10:1, 17–20:**

Jesus Sends Out the Twelve Apostles
9 And he called the twelve together and gave them power and authority over all demons and to cure diseases, [2] and he sent them out to proclaim the kingdom of God and to heal.

Jesus Sends Out the Seventy-Two

**10** After this the Lord appointed seventy-two[a] others and sent them on ahead of him, two by two, into every town and place where he himself was about to go.

The Return of the Seventy-Two

[17] The seventy-two returned with joy, saying, "Lord, even the demons are subject to us in your name!" [18] And he said to them, "I saw Satan fall like lightning from heaven. [19] Behold, I have given you authority to tread on serpents and scorpions, and over all the power of the enemy, and nothing shall hurt you. [20] Nevertheless, do not rejoice in this, that the spirits are subject to you, but rejoice that your names are written in heaven."

_______________________________________________

_______________________________________________

_______________________________________________

_______________________________________________

_______________________________________________

What is our role in exercising authority? On what basis? How does it work? What can we expect? Why?

**Read John 14:10–14:**

[10] Do you not believe that I am in the Father and the Father is in me? The words that I say to you I do not speak on my own authority, but the Father who dwells in me does his works. [11] Believe me that I am in the Father and the Father is in me, or else believe on account of the works themselves.

[12] "Truly, truly, I say to you, whoever believes in me will also do the works that I do; and greater works than these will he do, because I am going to the Father. [13] Whatever you ask in my name, this I will do, that the Father may be glorified in the Son. [14] If you ask me[a] anything in my name, I will do it.

# LESSON 7:
## TAKING AUTHORITY AGAINST THE ADVERSITY

_______________________________________________

_______________________________________________

_______________________________________________

_______________________________________________

_______________________________________________

**LIVE IT OUT AS THE CHURCH DID IN ACTS:**

In each of these stories from Acts, write out the important truths about how the disciples were used to overcome adversity. How did they exercise authority and what happened? How can we apply these truths to our lives?

**Read Acts 3:2–10; 16:**

2 And a man lame from birth was being carried, whom they laid daily at the gate of the temple that is called the Beautiful Gate to ask alms of those entering the temple. 3 Seeing Peter and John about to go into the temple, he asked to receive alms. 4 And Peter directed his gaze at him, as did John, and said, "Look at us." 5 And he fixed his attention on them, expecting to receive something from them. 6 But Peter said, "I have no silver and gold, but what I do have I give to you. In the name of Jesus Christ of Nazareth, rise up and walk!" 7 And he took him by the right hand and raised him up, and immediately his feet and ankles were made strong. 8 And leaping up, he stood and began to walk, and entered the temple with them, walking and leaping and praising God. 9 And all the people saw him walking and praising God, 10 and recognized him as the one who sat at the Beautiful Gate of the temple, asking for alms. And they were filled with wonder and amazement at what had happened to him.

_______________________________________________

_______________________________________________

_______________________________________________

_______________________________________________

**Read Acts 9:32–43:**

The Healing of Aeneas

32 Now as Peter went here and there among them all, he came down also to the saints who lived at Lydda. 33 There he found a man named Aeneas, bedridden for eight years, who was paralyzed. 34 And Peter said to him, "Aeneas, Jesus Christ heals you; rise and make your bed." And immediately he rose. 35 And all the residents of Lydda and Sharon saw him, and they turned to the Lord.

Dorcas Restored to Life

36 Now there was in Joppa a disciple named Tabitha, which, translated, means Dorcas.[a] She was full of good works and acts of charity. 37 In those days she became ill and died, and when they had washed her, they laid her in an upper room. 38 Since Lydda was near Joppa, the disciples, hearing that Peter was there, sent two men to him, urging him, "Please come to us without delay." 39 So Peter rose and went with them. And when he arrived, they took him to the upper room. All the widows stood beside him weeping and showing tunics[b] and other garments that Dorcas made while she was with them. 40 But Peter put them all outside, and knelt down and prayed; and turning to the body he said, "Tabitha, arise." And she opened her eyes, and when she saw Peter she sat up. 41 And he gave her his hand and raised her up. Then, calling the saints and widows, he presented her alive. 42 And it became known throughout all Joppa, and many believed in the Lord. 43 And he stayed in Joppa for many days with one Simon, a tanner.

_______________________________________________

_______________________________________________

_______________________________________________

_______________________________________________

_______________________________________________

**Read Acts 16:16–40:**

Paul and Silas in Prison

**16** As we were going to the place of prayer, we were met by a slave girl who had a spirit of divination and brought her owners much gain by fortune-telling. [17] She followed Paul and us, crying out, "These men are servants of the Most High God, who proclaim to you the way of salvation." [18] And this she kept doing for many days. Paul, having become greatly annoyed, turned and said to the spirit, "I command you in the name of Jesus Christ to come out of her." And it came out that very hour.

[19] But when her owners saw that their hope of gain was gone, they seized Paul and Silas and dragged them into the marketplace before the rulers. [20] And when they had brought them to the magistrates, they said, "These men are Jews, and they are disturbing our city. [21] They advocate customs that are not lawful for us as Romans to accept or practice." [22] The crowd joined in attacking them, and the magistrates tore the garments off them and gave orders to beat them with rods.[23] And when they had inflicted many blows upon them, they threw them into prison, ordering the jailer to keep them safely. [24] Having received this order, he put them into the inner prison and fastened their feet in the stocks.

The Philippian Jailer Converted

[25] About midnight Paul and Silas were praying and singing hymns to God, and the prisoners were listening to them, [26] and suddenly there was a great earthquake, so that the foundations of the prison were shaken. And immediately all the doors were opened, and everyone's bonds were unfastened. [27] When the jailer woke and saw that the prison doors were open, he drew his sword and was about to kill himself, supposing that the prisoners had escaped. [28] But Paul cried with a loud voice, "Do not harm yourself, for we are all here." [29] And the jailer[a] called for lights and rushed in, and trembling with fear he fell down before Paul and Silas. [30] Then he brought them out and said, "Sirs, what must I do to be saved?" [31] And they said, "Believe in the Lord Jesus, and you will be saved, you and your household." [32] And they spoke the word of the Lord to him and to all who were in his house. [33] And he took them the same hour of the night and washed their wounds; and he was baptized at once, he and all his family. [34] Then he brought them up into his house and set food before them. And he rejoiced along with his entire household that he had believed in God.

> [35] But when it was day, the magistrates sent the police, saying, "Let those men go." [36] And the jailer reported these words to Paul, saying, "The magistrates have sent to let you go. Therefore come out now and go in peace." [37] But Paul said to them, "They have beaten us publicly, uncondemned, men who are Roman citizens, and have thrown us into prison; and do they now throw us out secretly? No! Let them come themselves and take us out." [38] The police reported these words to the magistrates, and they were afraid when they heard that they were Roman citizens. [39] So they came and apologized to them. And they took them out and asked them to leave the city. [40] So they went out of the prison and visited Lydia. And when they had seen the brothers, they encouraged them and departed.

_______________________________________

_______________________________________

_______________________________________

_______________________________________

_______________________________________

What is true about the supernatural? How should we live this out?

> **Signs and wonders are normal and bear witness to the spiritual life. Read Hebrews 2:1–4:**
>
> Warning Against Neglecting Salvation
> **2** Therefore we must pay much closer attention to what we have heard, lest we drift away from it. [2] For since the message declared by angels proved to be reliable, and every transgression or disobedience received a just retribution, [3] how shall we escape if we neglect such a great salvation? It was declared at first by the Lord, and it was attested to us by those who heard, [4] while God also bore witness by signs and wonders and various miracles and by gifts of the Holy Spirit distributed according to his will.

# LESSON 7:
## TAKING AUTHORITY AGAINST THE ADVERSITY

_______________________________________________

_______________________________________________

_______________________________________________

_______________________________________________

_______________________________________________

How does the supernatural work? On what basis are we to experience this personally?

> **Authority comes from what is true and what He speaks by faith. Read Matthew 8:5–13:**
>
> The Faith of a Centurion
>
> [5] When he had entered Capernaum, a centurion came forward to him, appealing to him, [6] "Lord, my servant is lying paralyzed at home, suffering terribly." [7] And he said to him, "I will come and heal him." [8] But the centurion replied, "Lord, I am not worthy to have you come under my roof, but only say the word, and my servant will be healed. [9] For I too am a man under authority, with soldiers under me. And I say to one, 'Go,' and he goes, and to another, 'Come,' and he comes, and to my servant,[a] 'Do this,' and he does it." [10] When Jesus heard this, he marveled and said to those who followed him, "Truly, I tell you, with no one in Israel[b] have I found such faith. [11] I tell you, many will come from east and west and recline at table with Abraham, Isaac, and Jacob in the kingdom of heaven, [12] while the sons of the kingdom will be thrown into the outer darkness. In that place there will be weeping and gnashing of teeth." [13] And to the centurion Jesus said, "Go; let it be done for you as you have believed." And the servant was healed at that very moment.

_______________________________________________

_______________________________________________

_______________________________________________

_______________________________________________

How does wisdom play a role in our receiving His authority to exercise the supernatural? How does it work practically?

> **Read James 1:5–8:**
>
> [5] If any of you lacks wisdom, let him ask God, who gives generously to all without reproach, and it will be given him. [6] But let him ask in faith, with no doubting, for the one who doubts is like a wave of the sea that is driven and tossed by the wind. [7] For that person must not suppose that he will receive anything from the Lord; [8] he is a double-minded man, unstable in all his ways.

# LESSON 8:
## ATTACK OF SATAN: PERSECUTION

As we have dealt with these different adversities, there is one final adversity that likely will happen and will require a unique response. That adversity is persecution. Let's explore what persecution is and how God instructs us to react to persecution.

What does Christ tell us about persecution? Why is this important for us?

**Read Matthew 5:10–12:**

[10] "Blessed are those who are persecuted for righteousness' sake, for theirs is the kingdom of heaven.

[11] "Blessed are you when others revile you and persecute you and utter all kinds of evil against you falsely on my account. [12] Rejoice and be glad, for your reward is great in heaven, for so they persecuted the prophets who were before you.

________________________________________

________________________________________

________________________________________

________________________________________

________________________________________

________________________________________

________________________________________

What does Christ further tell us about persecution? Why is this element of persecution important for us?

**Read Luke 21:10–19:**

Jesus Foretells Wars and Persecution
[10] Then he said to them, "Nation will rise against nation, and kingdom against kingdom. [11] There will be great earthquakes, and in various places famines and

> "... if you're walking in the Spirit, you are living out the life of God with respect, with honor, and you are presenting truth and righteousness."

pestilences. And there will be terrors and great signs from heaven. [12] But before all this they will lay their hands on you and persecute you, delivering you up to the synagogues and prisons, and you will be brought before kings and governors for my name's sake. [13] This will be your opportunity to bear witness. [14] Settle it therefore in your minds not to meditate beforehand how to answer, [15] for I will give you a mouth and wisdom, which none of your adversaries will be able to withstand or contradict. [16] You will be delivered up even by parents and brothers[a] and relatives and friends, and some of you they will put to death.[17] You will be hated by all for my name's sake. [18] But not a hair of your head will perish. [19] By your endurance you will gain your lives.

Christ tells us more profound truths about persecution. What does He say, and what does this mean for us?

**Read John 15:18–27:**

The Hatred of the World

[18] "If the world hates you, know that it has hated me before it hated you. [19] If you were of the world, the world would love you as its own; but because you are not of the world, but I chose you out of the world, therefore the world hates you.[20] Remember the word that I said to you: 'A servant is not greater than his master.' If they persecuted me, they will also persecute you. If they kept my word, they will also keep yours. [21] But all these things they will do to you on account of my name, because they do not know him who sent me. [22] If I had not come and spoken to them, they would not have been guilty of sin,[a] but now they have no excuse for their sin. [23] Whoever hates me hates my Father also. [24] If I had not done among them the works that no one else did, they would not be guilty of sin, but now they have seen and hated both me and my Father. [25] But the word that is written in their Law must be fulfilled: 'They hated me without a cause.'

> <sup>26</sup> "But when the Helper comes, whom I will send to you from the Father, the Spirit of truth, who proceeds from the Father, he will bear witness about me.<sup>27</sup> And you also will bear witness, because you have been with me from the beginning.

__________________________________________________

__________________________________________________

__________________________________________________

__________________________________________________

__________________________________________________

Paul tells us what happened to him as a believer, regarding persecution. What should we expect, and why is that important for us?

**Read 2 Corinthians 4:7–12:**

Treasure in Jars of Clay

<sup>7</sup> But we have this treasure in jars of clay, to show that the surpassing power belongs to God and not to us. <sup>8</sup> We are afflicted in every way, but not crushed; perplexed, but not driven to despair; <sup>9</sup> persecuted, but not forsaken; struck down, but not destroyed; <sup>10</sup> always carrying in the body the death of Jesus, so that the life of Jesus may also be manifested in our bodies. <sup>11</sup> For we who live are always being given over to death for Jesus' sake, so that the life of Jesus also may be manifested in our mortal flesh. <sup>12</sup> So death is at work in us, but life in you.

__________________________________________________

__________________________________________________

__________________________________________________

__________________________________________________

__________________________________________________

As time marches on, Paul tells us the persecution will get worse. What does that mean for us, and how should we understand this for our times?

> **Read 2 Timothy 3:12–13:**
>
> [12] Indeed, all who desire to live a godly life in Christ Jesus will be persecuted, [13] while evil people and impostors will go on from bad to worse, deceiving and being deceived.

---
---
---
---
---

As time goes forward, you who are living godly (in the Spirit) lives, walking in the Spirit, living in the Kingdom of God, will be harassed. There will be deceivers. Expect that. You're going to be persecuted. It's at different levels. What does that persecution look like? Harassment, opposition. People who don't agree with us. They want to silence us in a variety of ways. They try to stop us from doing what we're doing. How can we stop them?

OUR RESPONSES:

As we consider God telling us various responses to persecution, what does He tell us here? What does that mean practically in our lives?

DUST YOUR FEET OFF AND LEAVE.

> **Read Luke 10:1–12:**
>
> Jesus Sends Out the Seventy-Two
> **10** After this the Lord appointed seventy-two[a] others and sent them on ahead of him, two by two, into every town and place where he himself was about to go. [2] And he said to them, "The harvest is plentiful, but the laborers are few. Therefore pray earnestly to the Lord of the harvest to send out laborers

# LESSON 8:
## ATTACK OF SATAN: PERSECUTION

> into his harvest. ³ Go your way; behold, I am sending you out as lambs in the midst of wolves. ⁴ Carry no moneybag, no knapsack, no sandals, and greet no one on the road. ⁵ Whatever house you enter, first say, 'Peace be to this house!' ⁶ And if a son of peace is there, your peace will rest upon him. But if not, it will return to you. ⁷ And remain in the same house, eating and drinking what they provide, for the laborer deserves his wages. Do not go from house to house. ⁸ Whenever you enter a town and they receive you, eat what is set before you. ⁹ Heal the sick in it and say to them, 'The kingdom of God has come near to you.' ¹⁰ But whenever you enter a town and they do not receive you, go into its streets and say, ¹¹ 'Even the dust of your town that clings to our feet we wipe off against you. Nevertheless know this, that the kingdom of God has come near.' ¹² I tell you, it will be more bearable on that day for Sodom than for that town.

_______________________________________________

_______________________________________________

_______________________________________________

_______________________________________________

_______________________________________________

What does this response say? What does this mean for us practically?
GOD SAYS: "I WILL DELIVER YOU. STAY STRONG, ENDURE, CONTINUE TO BE HONORABLE, RESPECTFUL, AND LOVING. CONTINUE SPEAKING TRUTH; LISTEN UNTIL YOU RECEIVE FURTHER INSTRUCTIONS.

**Read 2 Timothy 3:10–12:**

All Scripture Is Breathed Out by God
¹⁰ You, however, have followed my teaching, my conduct, my aim in life, my faith, my patience, my love, my steadfastness, ¹¹ my persecutions and sufferings that happened to me at Antioch, at Iconium, and at Lystra—which persecutions I endured; yet from them all the Lord rescued me. ¹² Indeed, all who desire to live a godly life in Christ Jesus will be persecuted.

_______________________________________________

_______________________________________________

_______________________________________________

_______________________________________________

_______________________________________________

What does this response say? What does this mean to us practically?

GET OUT OF THERE NOW.

**Read 1 Samuel 23:1–13:**

David Saves the City of Keilah

**23** Now they told David, "Behold, the Philistines are fighting against Keilah and are robbing the threshing floors." 2 Therefore David inquired of the Lord, "Shall I go and attack these Philistines?" And the Lord said to David, "Go and attack the Philistines and save Keilah." 3 But David's men said to him, "Behold, we are afraid here in Judah; how much more then if we go to Keilah against the armies of the Philistines?" 4 Then David inquired of the Lord again. And the Lord answered him, "Arise, go down to Keilah, for I will give the Philistines into your hand." 5 And David and his men went to Keilah and fought with the Philistines and brought away their livestock and struck them with a great blow. So David saved the inhabitants of Keilah.

6 When Abiathar the son of Ahimelech had fled to David to Keilah, he had come down with an ephod in his hand. 7 Now it was told Saul that David had come to Keilah. And Saul said, "God has given him into my hand, for he has shut himself in by entering a town that has gates and bars." 8 And Saul summoned all the people to war, to go down to Keilah, to besiege David and his men. 9 David knew that Saul was plotting harm against him. And he said to Abiathar the priest, "Bring the ephod here." 10 Then David said, "O Lord, the God of Israel, your servant has surely heard that Saul seeks to come to Keilah, to destroy the city on my account. 11 Will the men of Keilah surrender me into his hand? Will Saul come down, as your servant has heard? O Lord, the God of Israel, please tell your servant." And the Lord said, "He will come down." 12 Then David said, "Will the men of Keilah surrender me and my men into the hand of Saul?" And the Lord said, "They will surrender you." 13 Then David and his men, who were about six hundred, arose

> and departed from Keilah, and they went wherever they could go. When Saul was told that David had escaped from Keilah, he gave up the expedition.

________________________________________

________________________________________

________________________________________

________________________________________

________________________________________

For the story of Stephen, what is the final response? What might this mean for us, and how would we view this?

GOD MAY SAY TO CONTINUE TO SPEAK THE TRUTH. YOU WILL SUFFER EXTREME CONSEQUENCES IN THIS LIFE, BUT HE WILL PRESERVE YOU THROUGH IT AND BRING YOU YOUR REWARD IN HEAVEN.

**Read Acts 6:8–7:60:**

Stephen Is Seized

8 And Stephen, full of grace and power, was doing great wonders and signs among the people. 9 Then some of those who belonged to the synagogue of the Freedmen (as it was called), and of the Cyrenians, and of the Alexandrians, and of those from Cilicia and Asia, rose up and disputed with Stephen. 10 But they could not withstand the wisdom and the Spirit with which he was speaking. 11 Then they secretly instigated men who said, "We have heard him speak blasphemous words against Moses and God." 12 And they stirred up the people and the elders and the scribes, and they came upon him and seized him and brought him before the council, 13 and they set up false witnesses who said, "This man never ceases to speak words against this holy place and the law, 14 for we have heard him say that this Jesus of Nazareth will destroy this place and will change the customs that Moses delivered to us." 15 And gazing at him, all who sat in the council saw that his face was like the face of an angel.

Stephen's Speech

7 And the high priest said, "Are these things so?" 2 And Stephen said: "Brothers and fathers, hear me. The God of glory appeared to our father Abraham when he was in Mesopotamia, before he lived in Haran, 3 and said to him, 'Go out from your land and from your kindred and go into the land that I

will show you.' [4] Then he went out from the land of the Chaldeans and lived in Haran. And after his father died, God removed him from there into this land in which you are now living. [5] Yet he gave him no inheritance in it, not even a foot's length, but promised to give it to him as a possession and to his offspring after him, though he had no child. [6] And God spoke to this effect—that his offspring would be sojourners in a land belonging to others, who would enslave them and afflict them four hundred years. [7] 'But I will judge the nation that they serve,' said God, 'and after that they shall come out and worship me in this place.' [8] And he gave him the covenant of circumcision. And so Abraham became the father of Isaac, and circumcised him on the eighth day, and Isaac became the father of Jacob, and Jacob of the twelve patriarchs.

[9] "And the patriarchs, jealous of Joseph, sold him into Egypt; but God was with him [10] and rescued him out of all his afflictions and gave him favor and wisdom before Pharaoh, king of Egypt, who made him ruler over Egypt and over all his household. [11] Now there came a famine throughout all Egypt and Canaan, and great affliction, and our fathers could find no food. [12] But when Jacob heard that there was grain in Egypt, he sent out our fathers on their first visit. [13] And on the second visit Joseph made himself known to his brothers, and Joseph's family became known to Pharaoh. [14] And Joseph sent and summoned Jacob his father and all his kindred, seventy-five persons in all. [15] And Jacob went down into Egypt, and he died, he and our fathers, [16] and they were carried back to Shechem and laid in the tomb that Abraham had bought for a sum of silver from the sons of Hamor in Shechem.

[17] "But as the time of the promise drew near, which God had granted to Abraham, the people increased and multiplied in Egypt [18] until there arose over Egypt another king who did not know Joseph. [19] He dealt shrewdly with our race and forced our fathers to expose their infants, so that they would not be kept alive. [20] At this time Moses was born; and he was beautiful in God's sight. And he was brought up for three months in his father's house, [21] and when he was exposed, Pharaoh's daughter adopted him and brought him up as her own son. [22] And Moses was instructed in all the wisdom of the Egyptians, and he was mighty in his words and deeds.

[23] "When he was forty years old, it came into his heart to visit his brothers, the children of Israel. [24] And seeing one of them being wronged, he defended the oppressed man and avenged him by striking down the Egyptian. [25] He

supposed that his brothers would understand that God was giving them salvation by his hand, but they did not understand. 26 And on the following day he appeared to them as they were quarreling and tried to reconcile them, saying, 'Men, you are brothers. Why do you wrong each other?' 27 But the man who was wronging his neighbor thrust him aside, saying, 'Who made you a ruler and a judge over us? 28 Do you want to kill me as you killed the Egyptian yesterday?' 29 At this retort Moses fled and became an exile in the land of Midian, where he became the father of two sons.

30 "Now when forty years had passed, an angel appeared to him in the wilderness of Mount Sinai, in a flame of fire in a bush.  When Moses saw it, he was amazed at the sight, and as he drew near to look, there came the voice of the Lord: 32 'I am the God of your fathers, the God of Abraham and of Isaac and of Jacob.' And Moses trembled and did not dare to look. 33 Then the Lord said to him, 'Take off the sandals from your feet, for the place where you are standing is holy ground. 34 I have surely seen the affliction of my people who are in Egypt, and have heard their groaning, and I have come down to deliver them. And now come, I will send you to Egypt.'

35 "This Moses, whom they rejected, saying, 'Who made you a ruler and a judge?'— this man God sent as both ruler and redeemer by the hand of the angel who appeared to him in the bush. 36 This man led them out, performing wonders and signs in Egypt and at the Red Sea and in the wilderness for forty years. 37 This is the Moses who said to the Israelites, 'God will raise up for you a prophet like me from your brothers.' 38 This is the one who was in the congregation in the wilderness with the angel who spoke to him at Mount Sinai, and with our fathers. He received living oracles to give to us. 39 Our fathers refused to obey him, but thrust him aside, and in their hearts they turned to Egypt, 40 saying to Aaron, 'Make for us gods who will go before us. As for this Moses who led us out from the land of Egypt, we do not know what has become of him.' 41 And they made a calf in those days, and offered a sacrifice to the idol and were rejoicing in the works of their hands. 42 But God turned away and gave them over to worship the host of heaven, as it is written in the book of the prophets:

"'Did you bring to me slain beasts and sacrifices,
    during the forty years in the wilderness, O house of Israel?
43 You took up the tent of Moloch
    and the star of your god Rephan,
    the images that you made to worship;
and I will send you into exile beyond Babylon.'

44 "Our fathers had the tent of witness in the wilderness, just as he who spoke to Moses directed him to make it, according to the pattern that he had seen. 45 Our fathers in turn brought it in with Joshua when they dispossessed the nations that God drove out before our fathers. So it was until the days of David, 46 who found favor in the sight of God and asked to find a dwelling place for the God of Jacob.[a] 47 But it was Solomon who built a house for him. 48 Yet the Most High does not dwell in houses made by hands, as the prophet says,

49 "'Heaven is my throne,
    and the earth is my footstool.
What kind of house will you build for me, says the Lord,
    or what is the place of my rest?
50 Did not my hand make all these things?'

51 "You stiff-necked people, uncircumcised in heart and ears, you always resist the Holy Spirit. As your fathers did, so do you. 52 Which of the prophets did your fathers not persecute? And they killed those who announced beforehand the coming of the Righteous One, whom you have now betrayed and murdered,53 you who received the law as delivered by angels and did not keep it."

The Stoning of Stephen

54 Now when they heard these things they were enraged, and they ground their teeth at him. 55 But he, full of the Holy Spirit, gazed into heaven and saw the glory of God, and Jesus standing at the right hand of God. 56 And he said, "Behold, I see the heavens opened, and the Son of Man standing at the right hand of God." 57 But they cried out with a loud voice and stopped their ears and rushed together[b] at him. 58 Then they cast him out of the city and stoned him. And the witnesses laid down their garments at the feet of a young man named Saul. 59 And as they were stoning Stephen, he called out, "Lord Jesus, receive my spirit." 60 And falling to his knees he cried out with a loud voice, "Lord, do not hold this sin against them." And when he had said this, he fell asleep.